JAPANESE AMERICAN JOURNEY

THE STORY OF A PEOPLE

JAPANESE AMERICAN JOURNEY: the story of a people
by The Japanese American Curriculum Project, Inc.

Florence M. Hongo, General Editor
Miyo Burton, Editor
Andrea Kuroda, Editor
Ruth Sasaki, Editor
Cheryl Tanaka, Editor

Writers
Takako Endo
Florence M. Hongo
Sadao Kinoshita
Katherine M. Reyes
Donald Y. Sekimura
Rosie Shimonishi
Shizue Yoshina

Hideo Chester Yoshida, Illustrator/Designer
J Paul Yoshiwara, Graphics/Layout
Timothy K. Okazaki, Computer Technician
Suzie Okazaki, Photographs

Published by JACP, Inc., PO Box 367, San Mateo, CA 94401
Printed by Spilman Printing, Sacramento, California

DEDICATION

This book is dedicated to one of JACP's original Board members who inspired and gave of his precious energy to organize and assist us in our early years. Edison Uno, whose biography appears in the biography section, most dearly believed in the curriculum development work to which JACP has dedicated itself since 1969.

Reaching young students to inform them about the Japanese American experience as part of our pluralistic society was one of his highest priorities. To tell the many untold stories of our society was to fulfill his fondest dreams. Edison understood that in order to have a truly democratic society, the young must understand the mistakes of that society as well as its successes.

Therefore, many years after his most untimely death, we of JACP fondly dedicate this book to Edison Uno, civil rights activist, Japanese American image maker, dedicated teacher, and friend.

PREFACE

Since 1969 the Japanese American Curriculum Project, a non-profit educational corporation of Japanese American educators, has been involved with providing homes, schools, and libraries with books and other materials for the purpose of enhancing the image of Asian Americans in general and Japanese Americans specifically. Our concern for materials which tell our untold story has led us in the past to develop many educational materials. *The Japanese American Journey* is our latest effort.

The journey of the people of Japanese ancestry in the United States has been a story which is similar to those of other ethnic groups in the United States. These stories, herein, are woven with the same pride, courage, and deep sense of heritage as other minority peoples have. This is the story of determination to belong to a society which rejected our efforts to find acceptance.

The Japanese American Journey has been developed for intermediate grade reading, grades 5 through 8. This book includes only a small percentage of the stories of Japanese Americans who have succeeded in our society with courage and tenacity. This book by no means tells the complete story. The accounts chosen are about individuals who set out to succeed in our society in their own ways. For the Japanese in America, success was combining the worlds of Japan and America to educate children and to create businesses, families, and communities. It was also being free to establish pride in their heritage and to continue their culture in the United States. In this pursuit countless road blocks were thrown up throughout their journey.

Much of the material contained in this book was rewritten from the book *JAPANESE AMERICANS: the Untold Story*, by JACP,Inc., Holt, Rinehart & Winston, 1971.

Through the historical section, we wish to give you a sense of some of the significant events which took place in the lives of the Japanese in the United States.

In 1971 the historical section was developed by Stella Takahashi, Shirley Shimada, Sadao Kinoshita, Donald Y. Sekimura, and Edison Uno. For this edition it has been rewritten by Sadao Kinoshita and Donald Y. Sekimura and edited by Andrea Kuroda and Ruth Sasaki.

Through the ten biographies, we aim to personalize our history with the story of individuals who contributed to many pursuits in the United States.

Takako Endo developed three biographies, which are being published for the first time. They tell the story of the three agricultural kings: George Shima, Keisaburo Koda, and Kiyoshi Hirasaki. The biographies of Joseph Heco and Kyutaro Abiko were rewritten by Florence M. Hongo. The stories of Kanaye Nagasawa and Edison Uno, also original biographies, were written by Katherine M. Reyes. Mike Masaoka's biography was originally created by Joe Grant Masaoka and is rewritten by Shizue Yoshina. The Daniel K. Inouye biography was originally written and now rewritten by Rosie Shimonishi. The editor of the biographical and short story section was Miyo Burton. Additional editorial work was done by Cheryl Tanaka and Florence M. Hongo.

Through the short stories, we share with you three heartwarming tales that will further your understanding of the Japanese American journey. With the permission of the author, Yoshiko Uchida, we bring you the short story "Uncle Kanda's Black Cat," which first appeared in *Abra Cadatlas* for Addison-Wesley of Palo Alto, California in 1981. Steven Mori gave us permission to use Toshio Mori's "One Happy Family", written in 1944 for *Trek*, a magazine published in Topaz (Utah) Relocation Center. Valerie Pang's short story, "Gambatte," won our contemporary short story competition in 1984.

We must acknowledge the persons who assisted us in achieving our goals by providing information, assisting with the writing and research, reading manuscripts, and providing critical input and encouragement.

We recognize the assistance of Ko Ijichi for reading the manuscript of Kanaye Nakagawa, his great-uncle; Rindge Shima for reading the manuscript on his father, George Shima; Yas Abiko, for reading the manuscript on his father, Kyutaro Abiko; Ernie and Rosalind Uno for their help with the biography of Edison Uno; and Yoshiko Uchida for assisting on her biography.

Interviews were conducted with Mineko Sakai and Elsie Nakamura for Kiyoshi Hirasaki; Toichi Domoto, Waka Domoto, and Ken Takeuchi for George Shima. Japanese language translations to secure historical information were done for the original book by Hisako Kawasaki Yamauchi of Fukuoka, Japan. Nobuko Andrews and Takeshi Endo provided Japanese language research for the biographies. We also acknowledge the assistance of the Koda family in reading the biography of Keisaburo Koda.

We also acknowledge the permission of Yoshimi Shibata, of Mt. Eden Nurseries, in Mt. Eden, California, for allowing us to use his short autobiography, "My World of Flowers."

Lillian Pang of the book committee provided encouragement and suggestions during the development of the book. Other readers of the manuscript were James Okutsu, Asian American Studies, San Francisco State University and Jan Yoshiwara, Assistant Director, Student Services/Minority Affairs, State Board for Community College Education, State of Washington.

Illustrations and book design were by Hideo Chester Yoshida of Dekiru Designs, San Francisco. Layouts were by J Paul Yoshiwara of JACP, Inc. and Kenneth R. Okazaki. Suzie Okazaki was in charge of collecting and placing photographs.

With his permission, we are using the drawings of Jack Matsuoka from his book, *Camp II, Block 211*, Japan Publications, 1975. Providing us with photographs were Go For Broke, Inc. and Steven Okazaki of Mouchette Films. Other photos were from the collection of JACP, Inc. and private collections of book committee members. Computer technicians were Timothy K. Okazaki and Douglas W. Levitt.

We also acknowledge the invaluable assistance of the Hongo Express for fast and efficient pick ups and deliveries of manuscripts, photos, art work, and correspondence.

We gratefully thank the California First Bank for making it financially possible for us to undertake this project.

FMH 8/31/85

TABLE OF CONTENTS

With Liberty and Justice for All

1

A Broken Promise

When the class stood to salute the flag and repeat the Pledge of Allegiance, Shig stood just a little straighter to look as tall as he could. He wanted his classmates and his teacher to know that he was just as proud to be an American as they were. Shig was a Nisei, a second generation Japanese American. He was the American-born son of Japanese immigrant parents called Issei, first generation Japanese in America.

Shig was often asked, "Are you Japanese or Chinese?" He would quickly answer, "I'm an American, just like you!" He wondered why people asked such questions. His parents always assured him that he was American, but so many people did not seem to understand.

As he repeated the Pledge of Allegiance, he thought of the words he spoke:

"I pledge allegiance to the flag of the United States of America, and to the Republic for which it stands, one nation, indivisible, with liberty and justice for all."

What do these words mean? Shig thought. What do they promise?

Liberty . . . freedom;

Justice . . . equality before the law;

Not for a few . . . but for everyone.

Shig learned that Americans of all races, colors, and creeds are guaranteed these rights by the Constitution of the United States. This was the law of the land. He was taught that these rights could not be taken from him or anyone. The Constitution stated this.

All these thoughts were to haunt Shig in the months that followed. Soon America, the country of his birth, was to be at war with Japan, the country in which his parents were born.

THE CALM IS BROKEN

The month was December. People were busy preparing for the Christmas season. The streets and stores in the cities and towns were beginning to look festive. The day was Sunday, December 7, 1941. In the morning people on the West Coast were going about their customary activities when they heard the terrible news on the radio.

The bombing of Pearl Harbor in Hawaii. *U.S. Navy.*

"The Japs are bombing Pearl Harbor!" the announcers shouted excitedly, "I repeat. The Japs are bombing Pearl Harbor!"

The news of the attack came as a shock to most Americans. They could not believe that a small nation like Japan would dare to attack the United States. Like other Americans, the Issei and Nisei were shocked and horrified. But they were also afraid. It was not only a fear of military attack but also a fear of what might happen to them. The Nisei knew that because they were born in the United States they were American citizens, but would their white friends question their loyalty? The Issei, on the other hand, suddenly became enemy aliens. The laws of our country barred them from citizenship.

What would happen to Japanese living in the United States? Would Americans hear what was in their hearts, or would they see only that their faces were like the enemy's? Instead of going on rides or Sunday outings, Japanese American families stayed home. They listened to the radio, hoping that what they had heard about the attack was not true.

The weeks that followed December 7, 1941 became a nightmare for Japanese Americans. Fathers who were community leaders, Japanese newspaper editors and publishers, businessmen, Japanese language teachers, and religious leaders were rounded up by the F.B.I. and put in jails. Families did not know where their fathers were taken or how long they would be gone. For these families this time was a nightmare of fear and wondering.

Meanwhile, children went to school, fearful that they would be called names and be mistreated because most people still thought of them as Japanese rather than American. They were afraid to face their white friends. Some children wanted to stay home, but their parents urged them to go to school. Education was very important to the Nisei even at a time like this.

Teachers tried to help by telling students to be kind to their Japanese American classmates. Despite this, the Nisei students still wondered if white Americans would remain their friends. Some did even though it was not popular to be friendly with the Nisei. Despite the ridicule and mistreatment, the Nisei still felt a strong loyalty to the United States. As one boy said, "This always gave me the courage to go on."

DAYS OF FEAR

The weeks after the attack on Pearl Harbor were filled with uncertainty for all Japanese Americans. The loss of many fathers made everyday life for families difficult. A curfew and a five-mile travel limit kept Japanese Americans restricted to areas close to their homes. Families were required to turn in shortwave radios, cameras, binoculars, and firearms to the local police. Older brothers and sisters returned from colleges and universities to be with their families and to help care for family businesses.

The Issei were proud people. They had worked hard all their lives and obeyed the laws of this country. It was a terrible thing for them to be afraid. It was difficult and cruel for them and their children to be judged because of the way they looked.

In some rural communities, vigilantes terrorized Japanese American families. There were shootings, and even killings. Anti-Japanese groups used the isolated vigilante attacks as an excuse for demanding that all Japanese Americans be put into detention centers. This was like saying, "Put them all into detention centers so that they will be safe from criminals."

Newspapers, magazines, and politicians fanned the fear and hateful feelings towards Japanese. They said, "Send the Japs away and don't let them come back!" Some even said that all the people of Japanese ancestry should be sent back to Japan. Nisei who were born in the United States and had never been to Japan wondered how anyone could be sent back to a place where they had never been.

THE GOVERNMENT ORDERS

On February 19, 1942, President Franklin Roosevelt issued Executive Order 9066, which gave the Secretary of Defense the authority to select zones where

WESTERN DEFENSE COMMAND AND FOURTH ARMY
WARTIME CIVIL CONTROL ADMINISTRATION
Presidio of San Francisco, California
May 3, 1942

INSTRUCTIONS
TO ALL PERSONS OF
JAPANESE
ANCESTRY
Living in the Following Area:

All of that portion of the City of Los Angeles, State of California, within that boundary beginning at the point at which North Figueroa Street meets a line following the middle of the Los Angeles River; thence southerly and following the said line to East First Street; thence westerly on East First Street to Alameda Street; thence southerly on Alameda Street to East Third Street; thence northwesterly on East Third Street to Main Street; thence northerly on Main Street to First Street; thence northwesterly on First Street to Figueroa Street; thence northeasterly on Figueroa Street to the point of beginning.

Pursuant to the provisions of Civilian Exclusion Order No. 33, this Headquarters, dated May 3, 1942, all persons of Japanese ancestry, both alien and non-alien, will be evacuated from the above area by 12 o'clock noon, P. W. T., Saturday, May 9, 1942.

No Japanese person living in the above area will be permitted to change residence after 12 o'clock noon, P. W. T., Sunday, May 3, 1942, without obtaining special permission from the representative of the Commanding General, Southern California Sector, at the Civil Control Station located at:

Japanese Union Church,
120 North San Pedro Street,
Los Angeles, California.

Such permits will only be granted for the purpose of uniting members of a family, or in cases of grave emergency.

The Civil Control Station is equipped to assist the Japanese population affected by this evacuation in the following ways:

1. Give advice and instructions on the evacuation.
2. Provide services with respect to the management, leasing, sale, storage or other disposition of most kinds of property, such as real estate, business and professional equipment, household goods, boats, automobiles and livestock.
3. Provide temporary residence elsewhere for all Japanese in family groups.
4. Transport persons and a limited amount of clothing and equipment to their new residence.

The Following Instructions Must Be Observed:

1. A responsible member of each family, preferably the head of the family, or the person in whose name most of the property is held, and each individual living alone, will report to the Civil Control Station to receive further instructions. This must be done between 8:00 A. M. and 5:00 P. M. on Monday, May 4, 1942, or between 8:00 A. M. and 5:00 P. M. on Tuesday, May 5, 1942.
2. Evacuees must carry with them on departure for the Assembly Center, the following property:
  (a) Bedding and linens (no mattress) for each member of the family;
  (b) Toilet articles for each member of the family;
  (c) Extra clothing for each member of the family;
  (d) Sufficient knives, forks, spoons, plates, bowls and cups for each member of the family;
  (e) Essential personal effects for each member of the family.

All items carried will be securely packaged, tied and plainly marked with the name of the owner and numbered in accordance with instructions obtained at the Civil Control Station. The size and number of packages is limited to that which can be carried by the individual or family group.

3. No pets of any kind will be permitted.
4. No personal items and no household goods will be shipped to the Assembly Center.
5. The United States Government through its agencies will provide for the storage, at the sole risk of the owner, of the more substantial household items, such as iceboxes, washing machines, pianos and other heavy furniture. Cooking utensils and other small items will be accepted for storage if crated, packed and plainly marked with the name and address of the owner. Only one name and address will be used by a given family.
6. Each family, and individual living alone, will be furnished transportation to the Assembly Center or will be authorized to travel by private automobile in a supervised group. All instructions pertaining to the movement will be obtained at the Civil Control Station.

Go to the Civil Control Station between the hours of 8:00 A. M. and 5:00 P. M., Monday, May 4, 1942, or between the hours of 8:00 A. M. and 5:00 P. M., Tuesday, May 5, 1942, to receive further instructions.

J. L. DeWITT
Lieutenant General, U. S. Army
Commanding

SEE CIVILIAN EXCLUSION ORDER NO. 33.

Reproduced by Visual Communications

"any and all persons" would be excluded. Although the United States was also at war with Germany and Italy, this order did not affect German and Italian families.

On February 20, 1942, Secretary of Defense Henry L. Stimson carried out the President's Executive Order. Approximately 110,000 persons of Japanese ancestry, two-thirds of whom were American citizens, were ordered to leave their homes on the West Coast. Japanese Americans were never accused of any crime nor were they given a chance to prove their innocence. Even the Supreme Court, the highest court in the country, did not protect Japanese Americans. Except for the equally shameful removal of Native Americans from their homelands earlier in our history, no other group of people in the history of the United States had been forcefully removed from their homes.

The Nisei, who had lived all their lives in this country, could not believe they were being evacuated from their homes. They wondered about freedom and justice. What happened to the promises of the Pledge of Allegiance and the Constitution?

Families had no idea when they would be given notice to move. Everyday they looked for evacuation orders to appear on telephone poles and on sides of buildings. Everyone was anxious and nervous. They made no preparations because they all hoped to be spared.

When the orders appeared, there was very little time to prepare, often as little as two weeks. Then everything that they owned had to be taken care of; land,

Officer inspecting baggage of evacuees entering camps. *Library of Congress.*

Armed guards guarding evacuees entering camp at Santa Anita, California
Library of Congress

homes, furniture, tools, and equipment. There was a frenzy of activity. Many took advantage of the Issei and Nisei by buying their belongings for next to nothing.

Each family member was given an identification tag with a number on it. Smallpox and typhoid shots were administered to prevent an outbreak of epidemics.

Packing was the hardest part. Evacuation instructions stated that each person could only take what he or she could carry. This included bedding, linen, clothing, dishes, and eating utensils. Some people threw out things they should have kept, and packed things they should have left behind. Everyone was bewildered and confused.

When the day finally came to depart, everyone was taken to assembly centers on buses escorted by soldiers. It was a heartbreaking experience. Some not only left their homes and friends, but also their family pets. Many tears were shed as people sadly left their homes behind.

HOMES WITH BARBED WIRE FENCES

Japanese Americans were put into assembly centers at nearby fairgrounds and race tracks because permanent camps were not yet ready. When they arrived at these centers, they found the grounds enclosed by barbed wire fences. Soldiers were on duty at the entrances, and sentries with guns and bayonets were posted in the guard towers around the camp. It was a frightening sight.

The first day in camp was an unforgettable day. Spring rains made mud puddles everywhere. The rain drenched everyone and the baggage too. Rooms were assigned one to a family, regardless of family size. Some rooms turned out to be converted horse stalls. Linoleum was placed over manure-covered floors. Nails and cobwebs hung from the walls and ceilings. The smell of dust and manure filled the air. In some camps the raw lumber used for hastily constructed floors cracked and grass came up through these openings in the floor. Partitions between rooms were not adequate. Crying, laughing, talking, and fighting could be heard from one end of the barracks to the other. There was little privacy.

Except for folding cots that were used as beds, there was no furniture. Mattresses were bags of ticking that had to be stuffed with straw. There was no running water and no heat. Toilets, showers, laundry rooms, and mess halls were shared by 300 others. People had to form long lines to get food while hunger pains gnawed at their stomachs. For their first meal families sat at long tables on

Mess hall scene. *Jack Matsuoka.*

A classroom at the Rohwer center, November, 1942, when there was very little school equipment. Teachers sometimes had no pencils, paper, or books to work with at the beginning. *Photo by Tom Parker courtesy of the* Pacific Citizen.

Winters were cold; there was only a coal stove for heat. *Jacp, Inc.*

backless benches and ate beans, potatoes, and bread. Food was in short supply. By bedtime bodies were weary, and hearts were heavy.

One day the Issei and Nisei were free people. The next, they were prisoners, herded into concentration camps under armed guard.

The evacuees spent the spring and summer of 1942 in these primitive assembly centers. They prepared meals, cleaned tables and latrines. Additional barracks were also built for other evacuees who would be coming later. Doctors and nurses cared for the sick with crude instruments and inadequate supplies.

There were few books and materials, but volunteer teachers organized classes so children would not get behind in their school work. Games, sports activities, movies, and entertainment put on by the evacuees helped to pass the time. There was much to be done to run these new communities. Everyone had to make each day as livable as possible.

AGAIN TO MOVE

Toward the end of summer, rumors about another move began. This time it was said that the move was to permanent camps in the interior of the United States. Once again the evacuees were ordered to pack their belongings and wait for government orders.

When the day came to leave, the evacuees were put on trains with military police to guard them during the long journey inland away from the West Coast. They were both anxious and sad. Many wondered when they would be allowed to return to their homes, if ever. The trains used for the trip creaked with age. The gas lights failed to work properly and the heating could not be controlled. It was either too hot or too cold. They were not allowed to open windows or even raise shades. After the excitement of the first day, the rest of the trip was a nightmare.

Some evacuees were taken to Idaho, Wyoming, Utah, Colorado, and Arizona. Others were sent to permanent camps in the interior of California, and still others were sent as far away from the West Coast as Arkansas. There were ten camps in all.

At the end of the journey the evacuees found themselves in barren desert wastelands. Military police were on hand to transfer them from the train to buses for the final part of the trip. The evacuees entered the camps through guarded gates. Barbed wire fences surrounded the camps and sentries stood at watch towers around the borders. They were greeted by row upon row of black barracks covered with tar paper. Clouds of dust swirled everywhere. By the time the evacuees made their way from the bus to the check-in center, they were covered with dust.

Inside the hall they were assigned rooms, one per family. These rooms were 16″ X 20′, 20″ X 20′, or 24″ X 20′, depending on the size of the family. Six of

Going by train to inland camps. *Jack Matsuoka.*

these rooms made up one 120″ long barrack building. Twelve barracks plus one mess hall for meals, a central H-shaped building for latrines, showers, and laundry, and a separate "recreation hall" made up a block. A typical center or camp had thirty-six or more of these blocks. The blocks looked exactly the same so people got lost very easily.

A room assignment might look like this: "Block 11, Barrack 7, Room A." The rooms were unfinished and bare except for a hanging ceiling light, a closet, and windows. A thick layer of dust covered the floor. A canvas army cot, and two army blankets were furnished to each person. Later a pot-bellied coal stove was put in each room for the coming winter. There was no plumbing or running water except in the H-shaped building.

A SAD TIME OF ADJUSTMENT

It was up to the evacuees to make the rooms livable and attractive. The men made tables and rough chairs from scrap lumber and put shelves on the walls. They also made partitions in these one-room homes for privacy. The women ordered fabric from mail-order catalogues and made colorful curtains to frame the bare windows. Outside the barracks, gardens were planted. The tar-papered barracks were soon blooming both inside and out.

No one knew how long the evacuees would be held in these camps. This was to be their home until the United States Government decided to release them.

Meanwhile, there was much to be done to operate these new communities of 10,000 or more people.

A white project director was sent to each of the ten camps to act as a city manager. He had a staff of aides who were in charge of different departments. The Caucasian staff lived in a separate area from the evacuees and ate in their own dining rooms. They were paid Civil Service salaries and were free to come and go.

Many evacuees also worked in the administration department. Often they were better qualified for their jobs, but were paid a top salary of $19 a month. Others were paid $16 and $12 a month. The evacuees worked under the Caucasian supervisors.

The military police were the watchmen of the camps. They guarded the gate and manned the watch towers. At night they turned on flood lights that lighted the high barbed-wire fence that surrounded the area. The soldiers were armed.

LIFE MUST CONTINUE

Although the evacuees were forced to live a new life behind barbed-wire fences, they realized that there was much work to be done. As soon as they were settled, they applied for and were assigned jobs for which they had experience and training. Women helped in the mess halls although they had never worked as waitresses before. Young and old worked together to do all the necessary work. They wanted to live as best they could.

Students attended camp schools taught by white as well as Nisei teachers. High school graduates who wanted to go on to college were given permission to leave the camp if they could find colleges that would accept them.

Some of the elderly people spent their time hunting rocks and pieces of wood. They polished them and made interesting art objects. They also planted gardens in the sandy soil and made the barren desert bloom. For them the days were long and the future looked gloomy.

Living in one room made family life difficult. The thin plywood partitions between these rooms gave no one much privacy. Everything could be heard by the neighbors next door. Parents continually pleaded with their children to be as quiet as possible, so children often used this situation to get their own way.

Formerly, at home mealtime had been a time for families to be together. However, the parents who had to eat in the same mess hall with three hundred others found it difficult to keep members of their own families together. After life in these camps settled in, mothers always ate with their small children, but fathers often chose to eat at separate tables with other men. Teenagers preferred to join friends of their own age. Families not only missed getting together at mealtime, parents were unable to find any time to be together. Family control was all too often lost under these abnormal living conditions.

Nisei soliders of the 442nd Combat Team in France, October 1944.
U.S. Army Photograph.

IN SPITE OF EVERYTHING

The Nisei suffered many hardships and inconveniences because of the war. But the one hurt that gnawed at the Nisei from Hawaii and the mainland was that they were not treated like Americans. One of the results of the evacuation and removal was that, with the exception of a few who were already in military service, Nisei men and women were not being allowed to serve in the military. They were deeply insulted by this action. They had been denied the right to fight for their country in World War II.

Through their Nisei leaders, they asked to be allowed to volunteer as soldiers and to prove their loyalty to the United States. When this request was granted by Secretary of War Henry L. Stimson, they volunteered from Hawaii and the mainland in larger numbers than was expected. These men formed the famous 442nd Regimental Combat Team, which joined the established 100th Battalion from Hawaii. They fought heroically in Italy and France. Their motto was the Hawaiian expression, "Go For Broke" which means, "Give it everything you have!"

Another group of Nisei that helped the United States in the war effort was the soldiers who served in the Military Intelligence Service in the Pacific. These soldiers received intensive training in Japanese language so they could communicate with the enemy. They were able to secure valuable information by questioning captured Japanese soldiers. During the early part of the war, they were a closely guarded "secret weapon" of the United States Army. These Military Intelligence soldiers were in constant danger of being mistaken for the enemy.

Together the 442nd and the Military Intelligence Service won more medals than any other group of soldiers during World War II. The 442nd won more than 18,000 individual decorations for valor.

In 1946, in pouring rain, President Harry S. Truman presented the Presidential Unit Citation to the 442nd and the 100th. He delivered the following message:

"You fought for the free nations of the world along with the rest of us. I congratulate you on that, and I can't tell you how much I appreciate the privilege of being able to show you just how much the United States of America thinks of what you have done. You are on your way home. You fought not only the enemy, but you fought prejudice and you won. Keep up that fight, and we will continue to win—to make this great republic stand for what the Constitution says it stands for: the welfare of all the people all the time."

Brigadier General Frank Merrill in Burma with two Nisei interpreters, T/Sgt. Herbert Miyasaki and T/Sgt. Akiji Yoshimura. *U.S. Army Photograph.*

Topaz Relocation Center in Utah

Leaving the camps to work on farms in Oregon, July 1942. *Library of Congress.*

THE BROKEN PROMISE

The Constitution provides the rights of liberty and justice for all, but for Japanese Americans, the promise was broken. They were deprived of their rights to liberty and justice by imprisonment without being charged of any crime. For three and one half years while Japanese Americans fought in the courts, the camps existed. In spite of this, the Nisei went to war to prove their loyalty and to fight for the principles for which they believed United States stood.

In Pursuit of Happiness

2

They Had a Dream

Immigrants are people who are born in other countries, but choose to come to our country to live. Some stay for only a short time. Others spend the rest of their lives in this country. Immigrants come for many reasons. They come to learn, to work, and to make a better life for themselves and their families. This is as true today as it was hundreds of years ago.

The immigrants from Japan came to the United States with these same goals. Like all immigrants, they have helped make this country a richer nation. Their knowledge and skills have helped to build America. Their culture has enriched the multicultural environment of the United States.

THE DREAM

Japan is a small island nation across the Pacific from the United States. Although the area of the islands is no larger than California, it has a much larger population. Producing food for the people has always been a concern.

Since long ago Japan has had many fishermen who helped feed the people of her islands. They fished from the seas which surround Japan. Often fishermen in their small boats were blown off course by fierce storms. Their small boats were wrecked or blown far from shore and many people died. Those who were lost at sea were sometimes rescued by passing ships. Since the the ports of Japan were closed to foreign ships, these ships were not able to return the rescued men to Japan. One of these rescued fishermen was fourteen year old Manjiro Nakahama.

In 1841, Manjiro went fishing with four other villagers. A storm came up and swept them to a small uninhabited island in the North Pacific. Months later they were rescued by a New England whaler captain named William Whitfield. The ship continued on to Hawaii where the villagers remained to wait for a chance to return to Japan.

Manjiro, however, stayed aboard with Captain Whitfield. Manjiro learned English and went to school in Massachusetts. Ten years later he returned to Japan and became an interpreter for the Japanese government.

Another shipwrecked sailor was Hikozo Hamada, probably the first Japanese to become an American citizen. He was later known as Joseph Heco. His great adventure is told in Chapter Seven.

Since the early 1800's the United States government had been trying to secure an agreement with Japan so their ships could have another place to resupply and refuel on their long ocean voyages. However, since Japan was closed to most foreigners this was not allowed.

In 1853 Commodore Matthew C. Perry sailed into Edo Bay with four warships to secure a treaty with Japan. After two previously unsuccessful attempts, trade agreements were finally made between Japan and the United States in March of 1854.

After Perry's visit, in 1866 the Japanese government permitted its citizens to travel to foreign countries. At first only educated people were allowed to leave. The Japanese government was anxious to learn about western ways that would help Japan. They sent some of their educated young students to the United States and Europe to learn about ships, trains, guns, government, and trading. They returned to Japan to develop a railway system and a modern navy.

It was not until 1869 that the first group of Japanese came to settle in the United States. This group of Japanese was known as the Wakamatsu Colony. They fled the town of Aizu Wakamatsu in Japan because of the changing government. They were loyal to the former rulers and were fearful that they might be executed just as many others who were loyal to the former rulers had been.

This group of people tried to start a tea and silk farm near Gold Hill, California, which is near Sacramento. They were not successful, and, because they could not return to Japan, some members abandoned the farm to search for jobs. The grave of Okei Ito, a teenaged nursemaid to the family of the leader of the Colony, is one of the few reminders of this colony.

By 1884 there were about two hundred Japanese living in the United States. Almost all of them were students sent by the Japanese government. Some young men came on their own to study. A few of them came from wealthy families. However, most of these students had to work while they went to school. They worked in homes as houseboys, servants, waiters, and cooks. There, they learned to speak a little English.

BY WAY OF HAWAII

Hawaii was not a state but a territory of the United States at this time. Americans went to these tropical islands and discovered that sugar cane grew very well there. Workers were needed to grow and harvest the sugar cane fields.

In 1868, a group of Japanese were hired to work in the sugar cane fields. Many workers were mistreated. When the contracts ended, most of these workers returned to Japan and complained to their government about Hawaii.

The Japanese government stopped other workers from going to Hawaii. But the demand grew for workers on the expanding sugar cane fields. The Chinese workers who were there before the Japanese were slowly leaving the sugar plantations to start small businesses with money they had painstakingly saved. They were not content to remain low paid laborers for the rest of their lives.

For years the Hawaiian plantation owners tried bargaining with the Japanese government to get workers. In 1885, the Japanese government decided to permit workers as well as students to leave the country. Before going to Hawaii, these laborers had to sign a contract. This contract was an agreement that they would work a duration of three years for fifteen dollars a month. They also had to agree to stay on the plantation to which they were assigned.

The owner could choose to treat a laborer as an employee or a slave. Some owners allowed the foremen or men in charge to use whips and other kinds of cruel punishment on the workers. Some of these workers tried to escape. If they were caught, they were fined or punished.

Those who worked under better conditions stayed on the plantations even after their contracts ended. Then they were able to get more pay as well as more freedom to come and go from the plantations.

After years of hard work some of these workers were able to leave the plantations to start small businesses in nearby towns. Their small stores and

Wakamatsu colonists arrive at Gold Hill, California, June 1869.

Japanese men working in a vineyard. *Los Angeles County Museum of Natural History.*

restaurants helped provide the laborers with the kinds of food and goods that they had become accustomed to in Japan.

WORKING FOR THE DREAM

We have learned that the first Japanese to come to the United States were shipwrecked sailors. Next, came students, who were followed by the workers, who worked in Hawaii. For many, Hawaii was a stepping-stone to the West Coast of the United States.

Although the Japanese government did not encourage labor emigration, it also wanted to protect all Japanese who went abroad. The Japanese government secured agreements to protect the rights of these emigrants. It was aware of the bad treatment of laborers in Hawaii.

From about 1890, many young men left Japan to work in the United States. As they returned to Japan they told wonderful tales about the many jobs and opportunities which existed in that far-away country of America. This encouraged others to emigrate.

Thousands of young men worked on farms in California, Oregon, and Washington. Some worked on the railroads. Others fished in the waters off the coast of California. Still, others worked in lumber mills, mines, and fish canneries. Some worked in English- speaking homes, learning to use English and to care for an American home. There were hotel owners and shoe repair men. All these men were Issei, immigrants from Japan.

Most farm workers did not have permanent homes. They often moved from one farm to another during the harvest season. In the winter, when the farms no longer needed their labor, they went to the cities to work in American homes or in Japanese-owned businesses.

Most of the workers were hoping to make the quick fortune they were promised. For them, one year did not produce the money they expected to save. Although they were very thrifty, they could not seem to save very much money because they were only able to qualify for the lowest paying jobs.

Years passed, and still the fortune the Japanese had hoped to make did not appear. Most refused to return home without the fortune they had promised family and friends in Japan. Others wanted to stay because they preferred the freedom and opportunities of America.

NO CITIZENSHIP

There was one problem which Japanese and all other Asian immigrants faced that was different from other immigrants. By a special ruling, they were not allowed to become citizens of the United States. This was a very serious ruling because it meant they could never vote, work in government offices, or work in professions which required citizenship. Even more serious was the inability to protect themselves against the waves of prejudice that were to overwhelm them in the coming years.

A WIFE TO SHARE THE DREAM

When the Issei decided to stay, they began to think about wives and families. Most of the immigrants in 1900 were men. Some of them had left wives and children behind in Japan. They sent money back to Japan so their families could join them. Others went back to Japan to marry, then returned to America to stay.

There were many men who could not afford to return to Japan to look for wives. In those days, it took three months just to cross the ocean one way by ship. The time was too long and the cost too much for most men to do this. So, a system called the picture bride system was developed. The men sent letters to their parents or relatives. In these letters, they explained that they wanted to find a wife. When these letters were received in Japan, the father or uncle of the

Mareyo and Iku Tsuchiya wedding portrait, March 28, 1914, Oakland, California.
Courtesy of T. Endo.

groom would try to find a wife in their own village. They would also look in the neighboring villages.

From Japan, a letter would be sent to the future groom. In this letter would be the names of the women that his relatives recommended. Often, short descriptions and photographs were included. From these names and descriptions, the young man would make a choice.

After he had chosen the woman and she had agreed to the marriage, the two would exchange photographs and letters. A marriage ceremony would be held in Japan. The bride would then go to live with her husband's family until arrangements were completed for her trip to America. After six months to one year she would pack and leave the village to join her husband.

How lonely she must have felt as she left behind her family, her friends, and everything that was familiar. How excited she must have been on the ship's long journey. She was probably a little frightened, too. She was going to a strange, new country to meet the man she had married but never met. How often she must have looked at her husband's photograph.

When the ship docked, pictures and faces were matched. It was not an easy task, for the pictures were sometimes old or not accurate. There must have been

A farmer loads his wagon with vegetables to sell. *Toyo Miyatake.*

Mr. K. Okuma looks over his vegetable farm in El Monte, California, 1938.
private collection.

some disappointed meetings at the dock, but there was little choice for change. Both the bride and groom knew that they had to stay together. Often they learned to love each other as they joined together to establish farms and businesses and to raise families.

ISSEI IN AGRICULTURE

As Issei men worked on the railroads, mines, lumber mills, and farms, they looked for ways to make better wages. They took notice of the vast amounts of unused land around them. They wanted a chance to grow crops on this land. In Japan most of them had been farmers, but in Japan their farms were small plots of land. Here, they saw farmers growing crops on hundreds of acres. And they saw thousands more acres of uncultivated land as far as the eye could see.

Since many of the Issei did not have enough money to buy land, they agreed to grow crops on land with a landowner's help. The landowner would provide the land and some equipment. The farmer would provide his hard work and skills. When the crops were harvested, both the farmer and the landowner shared in the profits they received from selling the crops. This arrangement was called share-cropping.

In 1907 the Asia Company sold dry goods in Los Angeles, run by Bungoro Mori.
Courtesy S. Yoshina

Another arrangement was leasing. The farmer rented the land from a land-
ówner for a certain number of years. Each year the farmer paid the landowner
rent for the use of the land. When he sold his crops, the farmer kept all the
profit. Leasing arrangements were often made for five or more years.

A few men were able to buy land, but could not afford good farming land.
They often bought land which other farmers thought was not suitable for
farming. These Issei worked hard to produce good crops from sometimes hostile
environments. Where water was needed, the Issei dug wells or ditches. Where
there was too much water, they drained the water. Where stones and rocks lay,
they removed them. Trees and boulders were moved as these determined Issei
cleared the land for farming.

One Issei started to grow rice in the dry land of the Sacramento Valley. No
one had tried to use this land before. Other farmers thought he was foolish.
After years of work and many failures, he was finally able to grow enough rice
to sell. The land which no one wanted became very valuable. It was worth many
times what he had originally paid. He was so successful, other farmers began to
grow rice.

ISSEI IN THE CITIES

As more Japanese came to America and settled, Japanese communities began to develop. These communities were usually located in an older section of a larger city where homes and places of business cost less. They became known as Little Tokyos or Japantowns. Other immigrant groups established similar ethnic communities in large cities. These communities still exist in large cities and are an interesting feature of all cities.

The Issei looked for a chance to start small businesses. Some started small stores, where they sold clothing and hardware. Grocery stores that sold Japanese foods were very popular. Restaurants and hotels were opening up all the time. These restaurants and hotels served the newcomers from Japan, providing a place to stay. It was also a place where bosses looked for labor. Other Issei established shoe repair shops, laundries, and cleaning shops. Many of these businesses were successful, but some were not. The owners and their families worked long and hard hours. It was just as hard work as the work of their friends and relatives on the farms.

They stayed. Their children stayed. Next, let's look at the growing resentment toward the Issei as they settled in the United States.

With Malice Toward None

3

Years of Rejection

"Ahh..." The hot hot bath water felt good to Mr. Kimura. Carefully, he settled into the steaming wooden tub that he had built himself.

"How is the water?" asked his wife from the doorway to the bath house.

"Good, good," he answered softly.

It had been a long day of picking strawberries. Reaching under the flat green leaves with his fingernails, Mr. Kimura had snipped each deliciously ripened berry and placed them gently, one on top of another, into the basket. Now and then he straightened up from his bent-over position. Together in the hot summer sun he and his wife worked down the rows, bending low over the strawberry plants. They used a handmade carrier that held six baskets. When the baskets were filled with strawberries, they carried them to the end of the row and carefully placed them in carts in a shady place.

While Mrs. Kimura worked, she watched her four year old son, Taro. He played by the trees where his baby brother, Kenzo slept.

After the long hours in the sun, Mrs. Kimura's work was still not finished. She hurried back to the house with her baby to prepare supper for her family. She also prepared supper for the men who worked for her husband. As she walked, carrying the baby boy on her back, she planned the evening meal. As he worked, Mr. Kimura watched Taro, while Mrs. Kimura made supper and started the fire for the bath.

The year was 1908. Mr. Kimura, like many thousands of immigrants from all over the world, came to the United States with many hopes and dreams, but with little money. Mr. Kimura's enthusiasm was matched with hard work, careful planning, and saving. Like other immigrants from Japan, he was not satisfied with remaining a common laborer. He dreamed of owning his own land.

A strike by the Japanese workers enabled some of the Japanese immigrants, or Issei, to become sharecroppers. The striking workers had refused to harvest the crops until the landowner agreed to rent out some of his land the following year. Although many of the landowners were angry at the striking Japanese workers, others admired them for their courage. Some of these large landowners helped the Japanese workers start their own farms. Those workers who had saved enough money could buy land. Mr. Kimura was one of them.

Mr. Kimura grew up on a small farm in Japan. Japan was a small country

A family like the Kimura's working in a strawberry patch. *JACP, Inc.*

with a large population, and farmers had to produce a lot of food from a small peice of land. Mr. Kimura knew how to do this. Although he could not afford the best land, his land produced more than other small farms. Many small farmers in California did not like successful Japanese farmers like Mr. Kimura.

This resentment was one of the reasons feelings grew against the Japanese in California. When the Issei first came to the United States, they were welcomed. Many farmers in California needed workers, and the Japanese were skilled and hardworking. Later, the railroad companies of the West welcomed them too, for they found that the workers from Japan were dependable and energetic. Almost everywhere they went, the Issei were welcomed. They worked on fishing boats, in lumber mills, fish canneries, and in mines. However, as the Japanese began to own their own farms or businesses, they, like the Chinese immigrants before them, were no longer welcomed.

Immigrants from China went to the United States about forty years before the earliest immigrants from Japan. Many Chinese went to California during the Gold Rush to make their fortunes. Some did make fortunes, but most were less fortunate. Their mining claims were often stolen. Some Chinese were beaten and killed. Later, thousands of Chinese helped build the first railroad to connect the

East and West Coasts of the United States. These workers were underpaid and often treated unfairly. Americans did not understand Asian culture and life style.

When work on the railroad was finished, many Chinese stayed in America and looked for other jobs. Some began their own businesses. Americans were alarmed. They did not want the Chinese to stay. When the earliest Japanese immigrants came to the United States, laws had already been passed to keep the Chinese out.

When the Issei began to establish families and businesses, they too became the victims of discrimination. In 1901, the governor of California was already encouraging Congress to pass a law to stop Japanese immigrants from entering the United States. The law was not passed. More anti-Japanese laws were introduced in California in 1903, but these laws were not passed either.

In 1905 Japan defeated Russia in the Russo-Japanese War. Californians suddenly became afraid of the Japanese who were living in California. A headline in a San Francisco newspaper in 1905 read "The Yellow Peril—How Japanese Crowd Out the White Race." The *San Francisco Chronicle* published headline after headline of anti-Japanese sentiment. This stirred many San Franciscans into action. Some of them began attacking Japanese people on the streets. There were beatings and robberies by gangs of young white men. The attackers were often not arrested.

Mr. Kimura and other Issei could not understand why Americans thought they were so dangerous. The term "yellow peril" was used to frighten people into thinking that the Japanese were dangerous. "Yellow" referred to their race, and "peril" meant dangerous. The people who used these words to describe the Issei believed that the Japanese were planning to take over California and the West Coast of the United States. Some said that the Japanese were taking jobs away from white Americans. These accusations were not true because the Japanese worked at low-paying jobs that white Americans were not willing to take.

THE HATE GROWS

It was in this atmosphere of prejudice that a young man named Tom Yatabe grew up in San Francisco. Tom was a Nisei, a second generation Japanese American. He was in elementary school in the fall of 1905 when the mayor of San Francisco and the Board of Education decided to remove all Japanese students from public schools. They wanted to put the Japanese children into a separate school for Orientals. The parents of these children protested. However, before the matter could be settled, something happened in San Francisco that made everyone forget about both issues.

In April of 1906 a great earthquake shook San Francisco. Much of the city lay in ashes and ruin. Hundreds of people were killed. Others needed food, clothing, and shelter. Money and aid came from all over the world. About $250,000 came from Japan. The government and people of Japan sent more money to aid San Francisco than all the other countries combined.

Tom Yatabe remembers his sudden move from one home to another. Everyone was busy looking for a new home or helping others to find safe, undamaged housing. Some moved to areas where Japanese had not lived before. Many businesses also had to move. Some Japanese started restaurants that served American as well as Japanese food. San Francisco was being rebuilt.

It wasn't long before people remembered the "Japanese problem." Japanese neighbors were not wanted in white communities. Many resented the new Japanese restaurants that served white as well as Japanese customers. Japanese restaurants and businesses were boycotted by white people, who tried to stop customers from going in. Vandals threw stones and broke windows. Japanese laundry cart drivers were attacked as they delivered clean clothes to their customers. White parents once again became concerned about Japanese students who were attending the same schools as their children.

SCHOOL SEGREGATION

One month after school started, Tom and all the other Japanese students in San Francisco were ordered to go to a special school for Orientals. Because no one else seemed to listen, the Japanese parents in San Francisco protested to the Japanese Ambassador in Washington, D.C. Soon after the decision, the Japanese community set up its own school, with tutors who would teach the children in English.

The leaders in Japan were angry when they learned about the school segregation in San Francisco. This was a insult to them and to their people.

President Theodore Roosevelt heard about the school situation in San Francisco and sent one of his aides to find out what was going on. Japan had just defeated Russia in a war, and President Roosevelt had helped to make peace between Japan and Russia. He did not want any bad feelings between Japan and America. Ninety-three Nisei children had been removed from public schools. These students had not caused any problems in school. The President's aide thought anti-Japanese feelings were the main reason for the segregation in San Francisco.

President Roosevelt thought that the people of San Francisco had acted foolishly. He called a meeting with members of the San Francisco Board of Education. As a result of that meeting, it was agreed that the children could return to the public school that they were originally attending. In return, President Roosevelt agreed to stop further immigration of Japanese laborers from Hawaii, Canada and Mexico.

San Francisco Japantown in the early years. *Bancroft Library.*

Japanese were working in many jobs; here gathering potatoes on the Shima Farm.
Courtesy W. Domoto

THE GENTLEMAN'S AGREEMENT

In 1908 the Japanese Foreign Minister and a United States ambassador reached an agreement to limit immigration from Japan. Japan agreed to send only skilled workers to the United States. This meant that the thousands of laborers who had been coming to work on farms could no longer enter this country. This agreement was called the Gentlemen's Agreement.

Many people in Japan did not like this new agreement. They, like Mr. Kimura in America, thought it was unfair to keep workers out from Japan, but not from Europe.

Around the same time, the California Labor Commissioner made a report to the California Senate on the Japanese in California. According to this report, the Japanese farmers were planning to stay in the United States and were willing to learn English and become citizens. They were good workers, and their skills were needed in California. "They encourage their children to become good citizens, too," he reported.

The Senate condemned the Labor Commissioner's report. "The people of California," the Senate claimed, "did not want the Japanese." The Gentlemen's Agreement was only the beginning. They would continue working against the Japanese, and eventually, they would keep the Japanese out entirely.

POLITICIANS AND OTHERS FAN THE HATE

While Tom Yatabe went to school each day, he did not think of himself as a problem. But many people in California did think of Tom and all other Japanese people as the "Japanese problem." Some California leaders formed groups to help spread rumors and stir up feelings against the Japanese. They said that the Japanese people were going to take over California. They said that Japanese people could never learn American customs, and that they should not be allowed to marry white people. Many states had laws that prohibited such marriages.

Anti-Japanese groups talked to politicians, and tried to get them to pass laws against the Japanese. Feeling was so strong that a politician could get elected by making anti-Japanese speeches and supporting anti-Japanese laws. Many of these laws did not pass because they were unconstitutional, or because they went against agreements that the United States had with Japan.

However, in 1913 California succeeded in passing the Alien Land Law. This law said that aliens, or non-citizens, who were ineligible for citizenship, could not own land. The Japanese, like other Asian immigrants, were prevented by law from becoming American citizens. The Alien Land Law was passed to prevent Japanese immigrants like Mr. Kimura from owning land and becoming successful farmers.

A few Japanese tried to become American citizens. One such man was Mr. Ozawa. Mr. Ozawa went to high school in Berkeley, California. He read and

Work crew on George Shima's farm. *Courtesy of W. Domoto*

wrote English well and attended the University of California at Berkeley. However, in 1922, after a long court case, the Supreme Court of the United States ruled that Mr. Ozawa could not become a naturalized citizen because he was neither white nor black.

To Mr. Kimura, the Alien Land Law was another obstacle that prevented him from realizing his dream of making a good life for his family. By 1913 he had two sons and two daughters. Taro was nine years old. Despite hard work and careful planning, how could Mr. Kimura succeed when there were people who did not want him or his family to have a good life in the United States?

FARMERS MUST HAVE LAND

Under the California Alien Land Law of 1913, Japanese immigrants could not own land. Eleven other states passed similar laws. It did not take long, however, for Japanese immigrants to discover a way to buy land in spite of this law. Many simply bought it in their children's names. Their children, who were born in the United States, were citizens by birth and could not be denied the right to own land.

This is what Mr. Kimura did. So, at the age of nine, Taro became a landowner.

Although the Alien Land Law failed to stop the Issei from buying land, anti-Japanese groups in California did not give up. They succeeded in passing more laws against the Japanese. One such law prevented aliens who formed companies from buying land. Another prevented such aliens from leasing land. The Japanese farmers were determined to stay in America and work for their dreams. Small farmers, labor unions, and politicians in California were just as determined to stop them.

WORLD WAR I

In World War I Japan and the United States fought together against Germany. Even this did little to stop the prejudice against the Japanese in California. A few Issei volunteered to fight for the United States. They hoped that they could become citizens by serving their country during the war. However, when they returned, they were disappointed to find out that they were still not allowed to become citizens.

Even though Japan and the United States were allies in the war, movies made at that time showed Japanese people as being sneaky and untrustworthy. Taro did not see many movies, but he heard about them. He could not

Farmers enjoying some leisure. *Courtesy H. Yoshida.*

understand why Japanese people were pictured this way. Most of the Japanese people he knew were very trustworthy and honest.

After Taro graduated from high school, he helped his father on the farm. Although his parents had talked about sending him to Japan for an education, they could not afford it. He was needed to work on the farm. During this time, Taro's mother received a letter from her brother in Japan. He wanted to come to the United States. Although he was only nineteen years old, he felt that he would have a better chance here. So the family made plans to bring Taro's uncle over. They signed papers and sent money; but it was too late.

A FINAL ACT OF HATE

It was 1924. A new law had been passed. After more than two decades of hard work, anti-Japanese groups in California finally succeeded in getting the federal government to pass a new law. This law was called the Immigration Quota Act of 1924, or the Japanese Exclusion Act. It limited immigration from each country to two percent of the number of immigrants from that country who were living in the United States in 1890. So for every one hundred Italian immigrants living in the United States in 1890, two could come from Italy each year. Most of the immigrants living in the United States in 1890 were from European countries.

This quota system alone would have cut immigration from Japan to almost nothing. However, in addition, the law stated that aliens who were "ineligible for citizenship" could not enter the United States at all. This meant Japanese and other Asians. The Immigration Quota Act of 1924 completely stopped all immigration from Japan.

President Calvin Coolidge signed the bill reluctantly. Like President Roosevelt before him, he was afraid such an act would anger Japan.

It did. The Japanese government called the Exclusion Act an act of "international discrimination." A former United States ambassador to Japan said it was an "international disaster." Thus, anti-Japanese groups in California greatly influenced United States-Japan relations. This, added to other problems, eventually led to World War II.

Meanwhile, Japanese immigrants in the United States continued to work for their dreams. Cut off from their native land, and shut out by the society of their new country, they raised their families in isolated little communities. These communities were separate from white American society, and were a rich blend of both cultures. In the next chapter we will see what it was like to grow up as an American child with a Japanese heritage in the years before World War II.

To Insure Domestic Tranquility

4

The Lifelong Search

From the beginning of American history there have been minority groups who have been treated unfairly. For all non-white minority groups this situation has continued to the present time. These stories have been untold until quite recently because people have been unwilling to hear the true stories.

In the earlier chapters, we have seen how prejudice and discrimination isolated Japanese immigrants into small communities that were cut off from mainstream America. We learned how Japanese Americans were prevented from attending public schools. Japanese were prevented from owning land for farms and homes.

It was in this atmosphere that the second generation, the Nisei, grew up in the United States. What was it like to be an American child with a Japanese heritage? What was it like to grow up in a time when there was so much anti-Japanese feeling?

The Nisei child's life centered around the home, school, church, and Japanese community. The Nisei were encouraged by their parents and their community to do well in school, to respect authority, and to bring no dishonor to the family.

Nisei children saw their father's role as the undisputed head of the family. They were expected to be obedient to both parents. In return, many sacrifices were made for the children. Issei parents bought new clothing for their children, but not for themselves. Instead, they would mend their own clothes to make them last longer. They were concerned about the public image of their children.

Issei parents relied on inexpensive forms of recreation in order to save money for their children's college education. The family unit was a team. Each person in the family had a responsibility. Most of all, the Issei saw their children as the hope for all Japanese Americans for gaining acceptance into American society.

As with most immigrant families, speaking a native language other than English made communicating with others difficult. Most Issei were too busy to learn English enough to be fluent, so they usually spoke Japanese, especially in the home. Therefore the first language of the Nisei was Japanese. Once they started attending public schools, however, they learned English very quickly. After a time, parents and children spoke to each other in a language made up of words from both Japanese and English. They could talk about everyday things, but ideas and feelings were harder to share.

Even though the Nisei spoke very little English when they began school, they

An early Japanese American family.
l to r: Mrs. Masako Yoshida; Sachi, Shizu, and Doris Yoshida; and Mr. Toshio Yoshida.
Standing: Tadao Uyeda, 1936. *Courtesy H. Yoshida.*

soon began to excel in school. Issei parents thought it was very important for their children to do well in school. They were proud, and also wanted to instill a sense of pride in their children. One Nisei still remembers the shame of having to stand in the corner because he could not understand the teacher's English. Many teachers, however, regarded the Nisei as good students because they earned good grades, did not question authority, and were reluctant to voice their opinions.

As they became older, Nisei children were more often the targets of prejudice. They were ridiculed by other children because they looked Asian, or because they could not speak perfect English. Nisei children were often called "Japs" and their accent was imitated by other children in sing-song chants. They were often barred from swimming pools and social clubs.

Nisei found a rich social life through Japanese religious organizations. Here, they were able to participate in dances, sports, drama, and other activities from which they were normally excluded at school.

The family, church, and Japanese community formed a strong support system for the Nisei. Due to family and community control, there was a low rate of juvenile delinquency. Nisei children grew up with the understanding that their actions were a reflection on the good family name. They could not do anything to bring dishonor to the family. Achievements in school and the community were likewise rewarded and praised.

Worst of all, the prejudice and ridicule that the Nisei often met with outside the Japanese community sometimes made them ashamed of being Japanese. A Nisei child might be embarrassed to appear in public with parents who did not speak English well. Sometimes bringing white friends home was uncomfortable, for fear that Japanese homes were different and white friends might not understand the Japanese life style. Sometimes, the Nisei rejected Japanese things because they felt they had to try harder to prove that they were Americans. It was not easy to blend in like European immigrants.

Issei parents stressed the importance of a good education in hopes that their children might have a better life. However, college degrees did not always open doors for the Nisei. When the Nisei completed their education, they found that job opportunities were limited because of racial prejudice. College graduates were forced to work in family grocery stores or fruit stands while their white classmates went on to professional jobs. Education did not always assure the Nisei of jobs in their chosen professions.

Some exceptions were the fields of medicine, dentistry, and pharmacy. In these fields the Nisei were able to become independent businessmen in well respected professions. These were professions which were much needed by the community. They did not require searching for jobs, only the opening of one's own office.

A fruit farmer and his son in Placer Co. in California. *Library of Congress.*

In the previous chapter, we met the Kimura family. We saw Mr. Kimura's son, Taro, graduate from high school and go to work on his father's farm. Taro's younger brother, Tomio, was a very good student in high school. He wanted to become an engineer. His parents encouraged him, even though they knew they would have to make big sacrifices to send him to college.

Tomio did go to college. Every summer he returned home to help on the farm. After five years of study, he graduated with honors as an engineer. Most of his white classmates found jobs and started working as soon as they graduated, but Tomio could not find a job. He had very high recommendations from his professors, but, unlike his classmates, Tomio was Japanese. His Nisei friend, who had been trained as an architect, could not find a job either. His friend went back to a job as a clerk at a Japanese store where he had worked every summer while going to school. Tomio returned to his father's farm.

After the harvest, Tomio went to Los Angeles to find a job. The best job he could find there was in a fruit and vegetable stand in Long Beach. He heard there were jobs in New York for Nisei engineers. So, after he had saved some money, he went to New York, which did not have the same long history of anti-Japanese discrimination as the West Coast. He found a job and made many friends there.

A group of Nisei students at the University
of California, Berkeley. *Courtesy T. Endo.*

Meanwhile, Tomio's older brother, Taro, continued to work on the Kimura farm. He was increasing the acreage of the farm and was becoming a successful farmer with the help of his mother, father, and sister. He was also becoming a leader in the Japanese American community.

As part of his activities, Taro attended a conference in San Francisco. There, he met Nisei from all over California, Oregon, and Washington. They talked about the discrimination they all faced while looking for jobs after graduating from college. Some of the Nisei tried to join the electricians' union, but were turned down because they were Japanese American.

The Nisei were angry and bitter because they obeyed their parents and fulfilled their dreams. They had received a good education, but this did not lead them to success or good jobs. Soon, with the bombing of Pearl Harbor, the Nisei belief in the American dream and their faith in democracy would be put to the ultimate test.

The Continuing Challenge

5

Pursuing the Dream

In chapter one you read about what happened to Japanese Americans during World War II. You read about the internment camps, and about how Nisei soldiers proved their loyalty to the United States.

Japanese Americans fought three cases up to the United States Supreme Court to protest their unfair treatment during World War II. In December of 1944 the Court decided that it was unconstitutional to keep Japanese Americans in camps or away from the West Coast.

THE RETURN

Slowly, Japanese Americans began to return to their homes and businesses on the West Coast, and the camps were closed. For most Japanese Americans, the West Coast was the only home they knew. They were anxious to return to more normal lives in familiar surroundings.

Some Japanese Americans who had resettled in the Midwest during the war stayed there after the war. They had jobs and housing there, and did not want to return to the West Coast, where they were not wanted. Most, however, returned to the West Coast.

Those who owned homes returned to them. For those who had mortgages on their property and were unable to make payments on it for three years, the property was lost. Many sold or lost their personal belongings. People they had trusted with belongings did not properly care for them or abused them. For many their life savings were gone.

For example, one young Nisei had a piano which the family somehow wanted to keep. It did not qualify for federal storage because it was not really a necessity. So the precious piano was taken to a white friend for safe keeping. When she went to reclaim the piano, the family led her to a leaky shed where the piano had been stored for three and one half years. There was a family of mice living happily in the piano and the rain over the years had ruined the outside finish. Even the beautiful ivory keys had become unglued. It was not worth salvaging!

Many returning evacuees were forced to stay in churches and public buildings until

A hostel for returning Japanese opens in Pasadena. Takejiro Noguchi from the
Gila Center is greeted in May, 1945 by Miss Katherine Fanning, Miss Sarah Field,
Miss Marjorie Noble, and Mrs. Kenjo Kojima, the housemother. Hostels run by
public-spirited individuals provided a temporary asylum for the Issei and Nisei who
returned homeless to the West Coast. *Courtesy Pacific Citizen.*

they could find housing. It was difficult to find housing because there was a housing shortage, and because there was still discrimination against the Japanese.

The more fortunate evacuees returned to their homes; but some of them were greeted with hostility and violence. Some Japanese American homes were shot at, or set on fire.

One family told the story of how, in the country, they always pulled their shades before turning on the lights in the evening. They were in fear that someone might shoot into their home if they saw them clearly.

It was a difficult time. Japanese Americans were free, and they were home again; but the evacuation had destroyed a lifetime of work. For two years they lived in fear of violence and other forms of harrassment. The Issei were mostly in their fifties and sixties; it was too late for them to start over. With the loss of property and money, it was not possible to begin the kinds of businesses they had had before the camps.

THE FIGHT FOR JUSTICE

Since 1930 and especially during the war, the Japanese American Citizens League (JACL) had fought for fair and just treatment of Japanese in the United States. After the war, the JACL continued with greater effort to fight against laws that discriminated against all minorities, and to specifically seek justice for Japanese Americans.

One result of the JACL's efforts was the passage of the Japanese American Evacuation Claims Act of 1948. Under this act, Japanese Americans could ask the government to repay them for part of the losses they had suffered because of the evacuation. Unfortunately, the terms of the act made it very difficult for Japanese American families to actually receive payment. It was necessary to provide proof of actual loss.

Because of the confusion of the evacuation, most families did not have records to show what they had lost. There was also no provision for making repayments for the separation of families and the hardships experienced in camp. No amount of money could be repaid for the years of hard work that were lost in a moment of wartime hysteria. The people who did receive some payment, however, were paid only ten cents for every dollar they claimed. One farmer who had 120 acres of farm land before the war received $2000 for the loss of his land, farm machinery, and home.

The JACL also worked for passage of the Walter-McCarran Act in 1952. This act, for the first time, allowed people of Japanese ancestry to become naturalized American citizens. After this law was passed, thousands of Issei took the oath of citizenship. Some of these proud Issei had been in the United States for over forty years. At last they were being accepted! They flocked to citizenship classes and struggled to fulfill the requirements, proud to at last be able to fulfill their

In 1948 Japanese Americans were allowed to claim for losses because of the evacuation. Farm equipment sold at a loss was typical. *JACP, Inc.*

Nisei students pose at U.C. Berkeley in 1948. *Courtesy M. Hongo.*

lifelong wish. The Walter-McCarran Act also allowed limited immigration from Japan for the first time since 1924.

PERIOD OF SILENCE

For a long time after the war was over, many Japanese Americans did not talk about their wartime experiences. They were faced with the struggle of starting from the bottom again. They had to pick up the pieces of their lives, and raise their Sansei children, the third generation.

Japanese Americans found it difficult to talk about the evacuation and the camps. It was hard to explain an experience that took away your pride, especially since you had not done anything wrong. As a result, most Americans, and even their Sansei children, did not know about the evacuation experience. It was only something which they talked about among themselves.

After the war, Japanese Americans still had to face job and housing discrimination. Although it was easier for the Nisei to find jobs after, rather than before, the war, it was still difficult. For example, even after the war, it was hard for a Nisei to get those professional jobs for which they were trained, such as teaching and engineering. Areas open to Japanese Americans included gardening, the nursery business, farming, civil service, and private practice professions such as dentistry.

Over the years, the doors have been opening slowly. As more and more areas opened up, Nisei were finally able to find the kind of work for which they had been educated.

As late as the 1970's, Japanese Americans were found to earn less than white Americans with the same number of years of education. Even today, although Japanese Americans can be found in almost every field, there are still areas such as management that are not occupied by very many Asians. This will most likely change as the Sansei and the Yonsei (the fourth generation) come of age.

THE CONTINUING SEARCH

The long period of silence that followed the war began to end in the late 1960's. During the 1960's the ethnic identity movement begun by Black people in America began to spread to other minority groups. Other minority groups began to understand that they were not alone in their struggles for justice in America. The Sansei began to realize that they knew very little about their own heritage. They began to ask questions. Nisei still were not able to talk about the terrible experiences of their past. But there were a few Nisei who were able to talk. Little by little the story began to be told.

As the Sansei discovered the terrible injustices of their past, the feeling grew that the United States Government had never acknowledged their errors during World War II. Worse yet, the government still had the power to make the

In the early 1970's Edison Uno teaches about the concentration camps.
Courtesy R. Uno.

identical mistakes against other minorities. In other words, the government still had the power to imprison groups of people based upon a suspicion of guilt.

In the late 1960's, organizations were formed to fight against Title II of the Internal Security Act of 1950. This act allowed the government to imprison citizens in a time of national emergency, even if it could not prove that the citizens had committed any crime. After the strong efforts of the JACL and other supporting organizations, the law was repealed on September 25, 1971.

CURRENT ISSUES

The search for justice continues with the movement for redress. Redress means to correct, to repay. Many Americans, not just Japanese Americans, feel that the United States Government has never apologized or repaid Japanese Americans for all of the losses they suffered because of the evacuation.

One of the first persons to speak out for the need for redress was a Nisei named Edison Uno. He spoke often about the need to resolve the many issues which still remained unresolved concerning the wartime removal of the Japanese Americans. He was a civil rights activist. You can read about his life in the biography section.

The drive for redress began in 1976. In addition to the JACL, there are several other organizations working on this issue. It has taken many years and much energy and money. But each stride towards victory brings with it a strengthened safeguard for all Americans and their civil rights.

Another important issue in the continuing search for justice are the Japanese American internment cases. In 1942, two Nisei were arrested for refusing to obey the evacuation order: Gordon Hirabayashi, a university student in Seattle, Washington, and Fred Korematsu, a worker in Oakland, California.

The third, a Nisei lawyer, Minoru Yasui, was arrested in Portland, Oregon for violating the curfew. At that time there was a law stating that all Japanese Americans had to be off the streets by 8 p.m. The three men were convicted, and Hirabayashi and Yasui were put into prison.

All three insisted that they were loyal American citizens, and that the evacuation and curfew were unconsitutional. All three cases went to the United States Supreme Court. The Court ruled that, because of military necessity, the curfew and evacuation of Japanese Americans were constitutional.

In 1983, almost forty years later, the cases were reopened by a team of Japanese American lawyers. Each case was argued separately. The court has overturned its decision in the Korematsu case. For Japanese Americans, this was

L. to R. Gordon Hirabayashi, Minoru Yasui, and Fred Korematsu—the three principals in the internment cases. *Mouchette Films.*

A group of Issei being honored at a dinner. *Courtesy S. Okazaki.*

a great victory. The United States Government was on trial, and it admitted that Japanese Americans had been treated unfairly. At this writing the other two cases are still pending.

Another issue of ongoing concern to the Japanese American community is the care and support of the elderly. Japanese Americans are often called the model minority because so many seem to have succeeded in spite of prejudice. Yet, Asian elderly are among the poorest of all elderly in this country. One reason for this is that Issei, because of discrimination and the language barrier, worked at jobs that did not provide retirement benefits. With the losses that occurred because of the wartime internment, any savings which might have been for that purpose were also gone. In addition, with the handicap of the language barrier, they did not seek the social services which English speaking elderly can apply for easily. For the Issei elderly arrangements need to be made for translators which are not usually provided by most social service agencies.

Japanese American communities have developed programs to protect and assist the elderly with housing, health, social services, and recreational needs. These programs are run by Nisei and Sansei professionals and volunteers. Through these programs, Issei and older Nisei can meet with friends, live in familiar neighborhoods, and eat foods to which they are accustomed. The Sansei

Children dance in a festival parade in Los Angeles. *Toyo Miyatake.*

Nihonmachi Little Friends in San Francsico learn about their cultural heritage.
Courtesy Nihonmachi Little Friends.

have discovered a rich sense of identity and learned about history directly through this contact with the elderly Issei. Since the Issei are all those Japanese Americans who came to the United States before 1924 as young adults, they are quickly decreasing in number.

THE DREAM IS NOT YET REALITY

Japanese Americans have overcome great obstacles on their journey toward acceptance in American society. But the fight is not over yet. Racial prejudice is something that people everywhere will always have to struggle to overcome. There are many ways Japanese Americans are dealing with these issues.

Young parents organize to teach their children about their culture and history so that the children will grow up with a stronger self image. Schools have been organized in many communities for this purpose. Cultural groups have flourished in cities and towns. There are musical groups, art groups, literary groups, bonsai clubs, flower arranging classes in addition to the traditional religious organizations and athletic clubs.

The Redress campaign and the overturning of law cases will continue until resolved. Organizations such as the JACL are continually on the alert against the reappearance of anti-Asian racism. They realize that there is a common bond among all Asians.

On June 19, 1982, Vincent Chin, a Chinese American, was attacked and killed by two auto workers in the streets of Detroit, Michigan. They were angry about the competition from Japanese automakers and thought he was Japanese. The entire national Asian American community supported the Chin family's efforts to secure justice for his death.

Refugees from Southeast Asia are often the target of prejudiced Americans. They suffer from language barriers and lack of jobs just as other Asian immigrants have at times in the past. The Japanese American community is concerned about these issues.

These are but a few examples of issues which Japanese American face. In the next chapter we will explore in greater detail the meaning of the Japanese American experience for all of us.

To Form a More Perfect Union

6

What Does Our Story Mean to America?

In earlier chapters we learned about the shocking treatment of Japanese Americans during World War II. Then we learned how this terrible event came about. We learned how the Japanese came to America, just as all immigrants have come, full of hopes and dreams. The untold story of the Japanese in America is not a pleasant story. That is the reason most of it has remained untold. Now we need to look at how the Japanese American journey is really a part of our whole history.

Often we as a nation do not enjoy telling about the mistakes that have taken place in our democracy. It is important to tell about success and the principles of freedom, equality, justice, and individual rights. However, that is not the complete story. For many people in America, it has been a story of fear, frustration, hopelessness, poverty, despair, and disappointment. The important question is: How can we tell both stories? How can we, in spite of past mistakes, work toward "forming a more perfect union"?

Compared to other nations of the world, the United States of America is relatively young. We are just over two hundred years old. In the beginning our nation was established because Americans protested against the injustices of the British. Americans wanted to form a government which recognized the right of the individual to have a voice in government. Our country has survived many struggles for the freedom and dignity of our nation as a whole and for the individual. This is good. These struggles must continue.

As a minority group, Japanese Americans are a very small part of this country's population. Although few in number, Japanese in America are easy to identify. Because they have Asian features, they can be quickly recognized. Also, Japanese Americans are easily identifiable because they have names such as Tanaka, Kinoshita, and Takahashi. It is easier to discriminate against a group of people who look different and have different names.

The story of Japanese Americans has been untold for a long time. Many Americans do not know that they do have a history in America. Many Americans still feel and remember the hate of the early years of their experience. Many think that Japanese Americans are from a foreign country. They don't realize that Japanese Americans have been citizens of the United States for many generations.

The plaque at Manzanar in Owens Valley, California. *Boku Kodama photo.*

For over fifty years the rights and freedoms of Japanese people living in the United States had been legally denied. Their rights were also denied by custom—they were not allowed in certain schools, private clubs, public swimming pools, and golf clubs. All these events came into sharp focus on December 7, 1941, when Japan attacked Pearl Harbor in Hawaii. For the United States this was the start of World War II.

Before World War II, discrimination was practiced by law and unwritten agreements. When the war began, however, discrimination began to be called patriotism, national security, and military necessity. Japan was now the enemy. The history of discrimination against the Japanese made it easy for the American people to believe that the government was justified in forcibly removing all Japanese from the West Coast, regardless of whether or not they were American citizens. They were not given a chance to prove their loyalty to the United States.

When the evacuation order was issued, the Constitution became a broken promise to all Japanese Americans. Their faith and hope in the American dream was shattered. Japanese Americans paid a great price for the evacuation in lost property, broken lives, and broken dreams. This experience has become part of the Japanese American heritage. This part of our history has become a dark chapter in the history of America.

These chapters have unfolded the truth—that the evacuation resulted from years of discrimination along with selfish economic and political interests. If we learn from our mistakes, if we gain understanding and compassion from our experiences with minority groups, if we gain new insights in understanding and seeking solutions to inequities in our society, then we have a basis for a more perfect union.

The untold story of Japanese Americans is a lesson in democracy. To know and understand America, we must be able to see and understand her successes as well as her failures. To hide the shameful facts would be wrong for you, who ask to know all about America.

The challenge of tomorrow must include the telling of many untold stories that are all part of our American heritage.

Biographies 7

JOSEPH HECO
A YOUNG JAPANESE BOY
WHO BECAME AN ACCIDENTAL VISITOR TO AMERICA

The first Japanese to become a citizen of the United States was a young boy who came to America because he became lost at sea. His name was Hikozo Hamada, later to be known as Joseph Heco.

Hikozo was one of the first Japanese to come to America to stay. He was only a boy of thirteen when the boat he was on became lost in a very bad storm off the coast of Japan. For fifty days the boat drifted towards America. He wrote about this strange adventure.

Over a hundred years ago Hikozo Hamada was born in a small Japanese village. The people of his village were farmers, fishermen, sailors, and traders. Hikozo's father was a well-to-do farmer, but he died soon after Hikozo was born. In those days a widow with children had no way of supporting herself. Soon Hikozo's mother remarried into a family in the town of Hamada. So his real name became Hikozaemon of Hamada.

As children, Hikozo and his brother heard their stepfather tell of being in Yedo Bay (now Tokyo) in 1846 when ships from America arrived in Japan. The two American ships caused great excitement among the nobles and officers because they arrived in the bay against the wishes of the Japanese government. At that time Japan did not allow foreign ships to come into its ports.

Hikozo's stepfather was asked to join with the several hundred other guard boats to help surround the strangers. He told of his fear when he saw the strange visitors from America. Although none of the Americans were allowed to come on land, they stayed ten days. So they went away failing to get permission to begin friendly relations with Japan.

Hikozo's older brother grew up with an adventurous spirit. He wanted very much to be a sailor. In those days a sailor's life was filled with danger because the boats were small. His brother, however, soon convinced his stepfather of his desire to go to sea. So he joined his uncle, who was the captain of a large junk trading between Hyogo (which is now Osaka) and Yedo.

Every time Hikozo's brother returned home, he told Hikozo and all the villagers thrilling stories about his adventures in the far-off places of Japan. Japanese people did not go very far from their own villages in those days. They listened with great interest to his stories of the seaport of Nagasaki where foreign vessels came each year to trade. Nagasaki was as far away to them as Moscow or Paris might be to you now.

As time went on Hikozo became more and more anxious to follow his older brother as a sailor. He wanted to see those distant seaports and those strange white men who came each year to Japan. When he told his mother of his desires, she became very sad. She thought of all the dangers of the storms which surrounded Japan. Too many boats and people never returned from the sea.

She said, "Why do you want to leave a comfortable home and go to sea where you will surely be miserable?" She asked Hikozo to continue his education so that he could get a position in a good business in Hyogo. He followed his mother's wishes and continued in school.

One day when Hikozo was thirteen, a cousin who was a sailor came to see him on his way to visit a temple with a tour group. They were traveling by boat. The cousin invited Hikozo along. Hikozo knew of his mother's feelings about his going anywhere on a boat, so he suggested his cousin ask his mother for permission. To his joy his mother said, "Yes, as long as it is only to visit the Temple."

Hikozo was very excited to be able to see for the first time the strange world outside of village that he had heard so much about. They anchored at the port of Marugame and went on foot to visit the Temple of Kompira, which is a Shinto shrine. Kompira is a god of the sea whom all sailors worship. A Shinto shrine is a place where the Japanese people go to worship many gods and great ancestors. There are beautiful statues and gardens, and it is a pleasant place to visit.

On reaching the shrine at the top of the mountain, Hikozo washed his hands and rinsed his mouth with water. The Shinto religion required people to come to a shrine with clean hands and a pure mouth. After visiting the shrine and eating supper, the group returned to the boat. Since the tour group had rented the boat, they asked to go to other shrines. The captain agreed, so they went on to visit other shrines in that area. The entire trip took fifty-six days.

When Hikozo returned home, his mother was anxiously awaiting his return. She hugged him and scolded him for being away so long, then asked him not to go away again, as it made her very lonely.

As Hikozo went visiting to boast to his friends of his exciting adventures, a neighbor came rushing to tell him that his mother was very ill. Hikozo could hardly believe it, since he had just left her at home in good health. He hurried home to find his mother in great pain. They sent for the doctor, but he could find no cure for her mysterious illness. After a few days, she died.

Now, with both his father and mother gone, Hikozo was very sad and lonely. Two weeks after his mother's funeral Hikozo's stepfather returned. They both remained at home during the customary hundred days of mourning.

By this time his stepfather's boat had returned to Hyogo and was ready to go on another voyage. His stepfather asked Hikozo if he would like to go with him to see Yedo. It made Hikozo very happy to be able to go with his stepfather instead of remaining in Hamada with his aunt.

On the way to Yedo, the sea became very rough. The crew sought refuge in a port along the way until the weather was clear. While they were waiting there, a brand new boat arrived. The captain of the new boat, who was known by the captain of Hikozo's boat, invited Hikozo to sail on his new boat to Yedo. Of course, Hikozo was excited about sailing on such a beautiful new boat. The captain promised his stepfather that he would take good care of him during the trip.

Once in Yedo, Hikozo went with the captain to visit shrines and theaters in that great busy city. They could not see very much in a day's time because people traveled everywhere on foot.

Once the boat was loaded and ready for the trip home, it left without waiting for Hikozo's stepfather's boat to arrive. At the start of the return trip, strong winds came up so that the boat was not able to make very much headway. The captain wondered whether they should stop for the night because of the winds. Shortly the weather seemed to calm down, so they continued south.

About eight o'clock that evening rain began to fall. The wind began to blow so hard that the men had to lower the sail. The boat began to roll. The roar of the wind and sea made such noise that Hikozo was not able to sleep. When Hikozo looked out his cabin window, he saw angry waves which looked as high as mountains. He began to feel very sorry that he had left his stepfather's boat, and he also began to remember what his mother had told him about how miserable a sailor's life would be.

As time passed, the storm became even worse until Hikozo thought that every wave would swallow up the boat and the whole crew.

Hikozo prayed that if the gods spared his life, he would never set out on a ship again!

After a period of calm, the storm began to rage again. The captain ordered the mast to be cut down so that the boat would not roll so badly. The boat drifted helplessly with the winds until the storm stopped. The crew had to throw some of their cargo overboard to lighten the ship and drag their anchor so that the ship would steer better in the storm.

They drifted for about fifty days, praying every day for some miracle. Their food supply was sufficient; they were able to catch fish and had plenty of rice. As they drifted eastward, they tried to repair the boat as best they could after each storm. But the storms had hurt the boat so badly that the sailors were not able to sail it back in the direction of Japan. They continued to drift helplessly to the east toward America.

One morning a man who had arisen early to pray to his gods saw something white in the horizon. He hurried off to tell the crew. When they all came on deck, they saw that it was the tall masts and white sails of a large black ship coming in their direction. They looked with great surprise at the big ship as it came closer because they had never seen such a splendid one. Her officers and crew were on deck and appeared to be very different from any people they had ever seen before.

They were all alarmed at the sight of the strange ship, so huge and black, and the strange creatures on board who might be, for all they knew, not human beings at all. But they could not allow this chance to be rescued pass them by, so they began to shout in Japanese, "Tasukete! Tasukete!" Save us! Save us! The ship slowed and turned.

The Japanese crew began preparing to abandon their boat. They discussed the dangers of boarding such a strange ship. Their captain knew that their boat would only last a few more days because of damage from the many storms during the past fifty days. He was not prepared to die aboard his vessel when there was a chance to be rescued. So they abandoned the ship with only the clothes on their backs and some bedding.

As Hikozo and members of the crew came on board, each one kneeled and made a deep bow to show his thankfulness for being rescued. At first the officers and men of the big ship all looked alike to the Japanese. Most of them wore beards, flannel shirts, and black pantaloons with suspenders across their shoulders. The captain wore long boots into which his trousers were tucked. Most of the crew wore shoes, but some were in their bare feet even in the cold December weather.

The captain was lean and tall with sandy hair, beard, and a moustache. He was about forty years of age. He had something in his mouth at which he puffed continually, and he sometimes blew smoke out of his mouth as he walked back and forth on the deck.

The Japanese had never seen or heard of beings like their rescuers before. They appeared very strange to the Japanese because of their different physical features and clothing. All the men looked very rough, and the Japanese were somewhat afraid of them. But the crew was very kind to the Japanese.

After the Japanese had settled themselves on the ship, they explored it with great amazement. Through sign language they asked when they would reach land. Japanese ships were never allowed by law more than a few days' voyage from land. The captain said that they would reach America in forty-two days. The Japanese were amazed because they did not know that the Pacific Ocean was so big. They were also puzzled about how the captain knew that they would reach land in exactly forty-two days.

At dinner time the cabin boy of the ship came up to the Japanese and made a sign for Hikozo to follow him. He took him to a small room and gave him a piece of cake-like food (bread) on which he spread some oily yellow substance (butter) and on top of that he put some brown sugar. He told Hikozo to eat it with a bowl of soup. Hikozo did not like the smell of the oily substance, so he hid it in his kimono sleeve. But the soup tasted good, so he ate it hungrily.

When the rest of the Japanese asked what he had eaten, Hikozo described the bread and butter, and the soup. They were very alarmed because Hikozo had eaten meat of a four-legged animal (beef) in the soup, which was against the law of the Shinto religion. It made Hikozo very unhappy to think that he had made such a bad mistake. Soon after that time, however, all of them began to eat beef because no other kind of meat was served.

One morning Hikozo heard a loud scream. When he went to see what the trouble was, he saw the Chinese cook in the act of killing one of the pigs on board for food. Hikozo was horrified because these things were not permitted in Japan. He had never seen an animal being killed. When the rest of the Japanese heard about the killing of the pig, they began to fear that perhaps they would be next to provide food for the American crew. One day when they saw the huge amounts of food stored in the hold, they felt much safer.

The Japanese had not seen land for a hundred days when the ship sailed into San Francisco. The Japanese were not allowed to go on land while the ship stayed in the harbor.

Hikozo, as the youngest of the group, received special treatment. One man who came on board asked to take Hikozo into San Francisco to show him the city and to buy him a pair of shoes, as he was still wearing sandals. Hikozo saw the tall brick buildings and the horse drawn carts of San Francisco. These things were all very new to him, and he enjoyed telling his friends back in the ship about his adventures.

For one year the Japanese sailors stayed on board ship while arrangements were being made for their return to Japan. It was very difficult to make proper arrangements for the safe return of the Japanese because it was still against the law for some foreign ships to go to Japan. During all this time, the Japanese were treated with kindness.

Finally, arrangements were made. The Japanese boarded a different ship to go to Hong Kong. When they reached Hong Kong, they had to wait again to transfer to yet another ship. On this next ship they were treated badly. They were kicked and beaten for breaking rules that they did not even know about.

An American man named Thomas felt that surely, in a few years, it would not be so difficult to return to Japan. So, in the meantime, Hikozo could learn English and help the Government of Japan when relations between the two countries were opened. After much discussion, Hikozo and two other Japanese decided to leave the group to return to San Francisco.

Thomas arranged with a Mr. Sanders of the Collectors Office in San Francisco for Hikozo to become educated in English. Later that year, Hikozo sailed to New York on the way to Baltimore, Maryland.

In New York Mr. Sanders showed him how a telegraph worked. Hikozo could hardly believe that a message could be sent and received on a wire. He was quite sure that Mr. Sanders was making fun of him. Mr. Sanders said that he would wire his brother-in-law in Baltimore to meet them with a carriage at the train station.

He told Hikozo they would ride a steam engine train to go from New York to Baltimore. Hikozo thought again that Mr. Sanders was joking about a train that would travel at forty miles an hour. He only knew the speed of a horse or a ship. But when they took a seat in a carriage with a steam engine in front, it began to snort and puff and move. It moved slowly at first, but after a while it moved so fast that they could hardly see the scenery clearly. When they reached Baltimore, Mr. Sanders' brother-in- law was waiting for them with a carriage, just as he had promised.

Next, Mr. Sanders took Hikozo with him to Washington, D.C., to call on the President of the United States. When they arrived at the White House, a man announced their arrival, and Mr. Sanders and Hikozo were taken into a room where the President was sitting, writing.

When the President saw them, he stood up and shook hands with Mr. Sanders and Hikozo. Hikozo could not understand how this man, dressed in a plain suit just like Mr. Sanders, could possibly be the President of this great nation. In Japan the Emperor was treated with such honor that common people were not even allowed to look upon him, or touch him or talk to him. Why was it that he was not guarded by soldiers and surrounded by attendants? Why did he wear such plain clothes? And how was it that Mr. Sanders, a plain citizen, could shake hands and speak to this man as an equal?

Hikozo wondered about these things because he did not understand the kind of government that America had. Hikozo asked Mr. Sanders again and again who this man was, because he could not believe that the President of such a great country could be treated as the equal of any of its citizens.

Soon after this time, Hikozo chose for himself the English name Joseph, because it sounded pleasant to him. After that time, he was called Joseph Heco and became a citizen of the United States.

After nine years, Joseph Heco returned to Japan to become an interpreter between the government of America and the government of Japan, but he did so as an American citizen. He remained in Japan the rest of his life to promote good relations between Japan and America. Joseph Heco was an extraordinary man who used his experience to bring about better understanding between the country of his birth and the country of his choosing.

KANAYE NAGASAWA
SAMURAI OF THE VINEYARDS

Today California is famous throughout the world for its fine wines. In the late 1800's, Kanaye Nagasawa was the master of one of California's best known vineyards. But he did not set out to become a famous winemaker.

In Japan during the period of the Shoguns, a young samurai named Kanaye Nagasawa set out for Europe to study Western government and technology. In 1852, he was born as Hikosuke Isonaga in Kagoshima. His samurai father was an important member of the Satsuma clan which ruled the Southern part of Japan.

For 250 years, Japan had been under military rule by the Tokugawa family, who forced Japan to be isolated from the rest of the world. Travel beyond Japanese shores was strictly forbidden by the Tokugawa Shogun.

While Kanaye was growing up, the Satsuma clan became increasingly unhappy with the long and hard military rule of Japan. The Satsuma clan wanted to restore the country to its rightful ruler, the Emperor. They also wanted to learn about the new changes which were rapidly taking place in Europe and America. They sensed that the time was near for Japan to open its doors to the outside world. The Satsuma clan wanted to be ready to help Japan join the world of nations. What was sorely needed was a group of young Japanese leaders educated in Western ways who could step in to lead a new government which was about to be formed.

Shimazu, the Lord of Satsuma, decided on a bold move. He would send a group of their promising young samurai to Europe. They would learn as much as they could about Western government, science and technology. Fifteen young men between the ages of thirteen and nineteen, along with four adults, were carefully chosen for this mission.

In order to conceal the secret mission each samurai was given a new name. The students with their new names were given special subjects to study. As Kanaye Nagasawa, he was assigned to study ship building.

In April of 1865, the group of nineteen secretly left Japan on their first voyage to Europe. After two months of switching from vessel to vessel they arrived in England and established London as their home. The students wasted no time in beginning their studies.

Kanaye, at thirteen, was the youngest in the group. Since he was too young to enter the University of London, he was sent to Aberdeen, Scotland to study English. There Kanaye was able to compare his upbringing with that of the people of Aberdeen. He experienced being treated as different because he was Japanese, but that did not force him to abandon his samurai heritage.

Back in Japan, the Satsuma clan was facing large debts due to the wars with the Tokugawa government. As a result, Lord Shimazu was forced to call back all but six of the original nineteen who were sent to Europe. Kanaye was one of the six who were left behind. Suspecting that the remainder of the group would be called back to Japan in a short time too, the remaining six decided to leave England to tour other countries. Two from the group went to America.

During their stay in the United States these two students met a kind gentleman who later greatly influenced Kanaye's life. This man's name was Thomas Lake Harris, founder of a religious cult which he called "Brotherhood of the New Life."

The students were impressed by this man and his religion. They found certain similarities between Harris' religion and Confucianism and Shintoism which were part of their earlier training. Thomas Harris, upon hearing that the Satsuma Clan could no longer support the six students, offered to help them by promising them continued education in exchange for labor.

The two students returned to London where they shared Harris' offer with the other students. Thomas Harris himself later came to England to persuade the students to follow him to the New World. Thus, in August of 1867 Kanaye and his fellow students left London for Harris' colony in America.

The students' first home was on the 2,000 acre Salem-on-Erie vineyard in New York where Thomas Harris cultivated grapes for wine. For the samurai students, working in the fields was difficult, as it was not what they had been trained to do. In a short time all of the students except Kanaye returned to Japan where they later became ambassadors and key leaders in the new government.

Kanaye, who chose to remain in the United States, set out to learn as much as he could about cultivating grapes and making wine. He worked in the vineyards with a viticulturist and vintner, Dr. John Hyde, who had joined the Brotherhood. From Dr. Hyde, Kanaye learned much and gained invaluable experience in the art of wine making.

As the years went by, Thomas Harris became unhappy with the cold weather of New York. He had heard about California as a suitable place to grow wine grapes. In fact, California was quickly becoming the center for wine making in the country.

With the opening of the transcontinental railroad, Harris decided to move to California. By this time, Kanaye, at the age of 23, was an experienced grape grower. He was happy at the thought of growing new grape vines and putting into use the methods he learned in New York.

In the Spring of 1875, eight years after arriving in the United States, Kanaye, together with Mr. Harris and a few others boarded the train for Oakland, California. The site which they chose to cultivate their new vineyard was on the hills surrounding Santa Rosa, fifty miles north of San Francisco. There, Mr. Harris bought 400 acres for $50.00 an acre. The estate eventually grew to 2,000 acres through additional purchases. Of this 500 acres were in grapes.

Mr. Harris did not rush into growing grapes. First, he built three splendid homes to house his family, members of the Brotherhood and a library. These buildings were elaborately decorated with the finest of materials and furnishings. Kanaye was to host many notables from California and throughout the country in these mansions.

"Fountain Grove" was the name given to the colony. The planting of grape vines and the building of a winery began four years after Harris' arrival in California. Members who worked for the Brotherhood received no salary.

Kanaye managed the vineyard and was the brewmaster. The wine made was sold under the label "Fountain Grove" with headquarters in New York. The wines were shipped directly to New York for distribution to Europe and Japan.

By 1880, Kanaye became the private secretary to Harris. But in 1892, Harris and his family returned to New York. Upon his departure, Harris left the total management of the winery to Kanaye who was then 40 years old.

When Mr. Harris died in 1906, Kanaye became the master of Fountain Grove. Once free from his responsibilities to Mr. Harris, Kanaye was able to spend much of his time on his greatest interest—improving the vineyards and the wines. Kanaye was a friend of Luther Burbank and Dr. Frederick Bioletti of the

Kanaye Nakazawa third from left with friends. *Bancroft Library.*

University of California, Davis, and worked with them on experiments in wine making.

Kanaye Nagasawa became a recognized wine expert and shared his knowledge with his friends. With his new role as an enterprising businessman, Kanaye entred his wines for competition. At the height of wine making, Fountain Grove wine was among the top ten labels distributed throughout the country. Kanaye was selected and served as a judge for wines aat the 1915 Panama-Pacific Exposition in San Francisco.

Kanaye made few trips back to his native Japan. By then Japan had changed from a feudal society to a modern nation. His last visit was in 1923. During the years at Fountain Grove, Kanaye received relatives from Japan who came and stayed. One of them was Hiro Ijichi, wife of his nephew, Tomoki. She served as his hostess and housekeeper because Kanaye never married.

The Japanese who lived and worked around San Francisco knew and respected Kanaye. One of his good friends was George Shima who became known as the Potato King.

In 1920 the Prohibition Amendment to the Constitution was passed. This law banned alcoholic beverages in the United States. Wine making at Fountain Grove was forced to come to an end.

Kanaye spent 59 years at Fountain Grove. He was highly respected in Santa Rosa where he was known as "The Prince".

On March 1, 1934, eleven days before his 83rd birthday, Kanaye Nagasawa quietly passed away. Because of the 1913 Alien Land Law he was not able to leave his property to his heirs. The Fountain Grove vineyard and what was left of it was later sold and the proceeds divided among his lawyer and his relatives.

His life journey led him to California where he pioneered and prospered in California's wine industry. Kanaye Nagasawa was a forerunner of the many Japanese immigrants who later arrived in the United States to make many important contributions to the development of our country.

Today, fifty years after Kanaye's passing, the young samurai turned Issei pioneer has not been forgotten by those who visit Fountain Grove. A bronze plaque in Kanaye's memory may be found at the entrance to the Round Barn, the only building left of the historic winery. It says simply:

Built in 1899 by Kanaye Nagasawa
Born in Kagoshima, Japan 1852
Died in Santa Rosa, California 1934
Samurai of Satsuma (Kagoshima), Japan
Prominent Sonoma County Viticulturalist-Enologist and
Pioneer of Japan Relationships 1875-1934
"Samurai Spirit in California"

KYUTARO ABIKO
A MAN WITH A DREAM
FOR THE JAPANESE IN AMERICA

Kyutaro Abiko was one of the many people who came to America long ago to make their dreams come true. He spent his life working for the Japanese people here in America. Mr. Abiko was one of the earliest immigrants of Japanese ancestry to come to America.

Kyutaro Abiko was born in 1865, in a village in Niigata on the Japan Sea side of the main island of Honshu. Kyutaro's mother died when he was born, so his grandfather took him in.

At that time, most people in Japan did not know much about other lands around the world. Japan had just begun again to trade with foreign nations. As Kyutaro grew up, he heard stories from people in his village who had talked to travelers. He heard about the distant city of Tokyo, the largest city in Japan. He heard about the great ships which visited the harbors. These ships, he was told, puffed great clouds of black smoke and did not need the wind to move. Kyutaro only knew about ships that sailed with the wind.

Even more exciting were the stories of what these ships brought to Japan. They brought cargoes that were beyond Kyutaro's wildest imagination. It was said that in the cargo were machines which did things men or animals could not do. The men who were on these ships were strange men with pale faces from a land called America.

When Kyutaro was only seventeen years old, he ran away from home to go to Tokyo. He wanted to see for himself all the things he had heard about. Tokyo turned out to be the exciting city Kyutaro had imagined. There he met many different people and saw many different things.

Kyutaro yearned to go to the lands from which the ships came, but there was a law in Japan which forbade the Japanese from going to foreign lands. Students were an exception, however. They were allowed to go because they could learn things which would be useful in Japan. They might learn how to develop new industries or how to grow certain food better. Kyutaro decided to become a student and enrolled in school.

Kyutaro thought of America as a place where the Japanese could go to realize certain dreams. He had heard of the great open spaces in America and the freedom to choose what a person wanted to do. Japan, on the other hand, was very crowded and had a system which did not give people the freedom to become what they wanted to be. People from all over the world wanted to go to America for those very same reasons.

When, in 1885, Japan finally passed a law which allowed her people to leave for foreign lands, Kyutaro boarded a ship headed for America. He was twenty years old, and he came to America to realize his dreams. It took every bit of the money he had saved to pay for his boat passage to San Francisco. When he arrived, he had only three dollars in his pockets.

Kyutaro found a job in an English-speaking home in San Francisco. He helped with the chores in return for a place to eat and sleep. There, he learned about American foods and customs.

While he had a job and a place to stay, Kyutaro could go to school to learn English. He started out in a class where the children were ten years younger than he. Some of them giggled and laughed at the idea of a twenty-year-old youth in their class. The eager youth ignored the laughter and studied hard.

Kyutaro went to the old Lincoln Grammar School in San Francisco and to Boys' High School. His friends could not pronounce his name, so they called him Kyu ("q"), which was short for Kyutaro. After finishing high school, Kyutaro continued on to the University of California at Berkeley.

The time came for Kyutaro to go out into the world. He stopped being a student and became the adult Mr. Abiko. He continued in his search for a place in his new adult world.

First he tried a hand laundry business which did not do very well. Then he operated a restaurant. He thought it might be a good business because many single men were working on the West Coast at that time, and they needed a place to eat. But his restaurant did not succeed. His restaurant served meals for ten cents with free bread on the side. His penniless friends would come to eat only the free bread, putting sugar on it when there was no butter. Mr. Abiko could not go on, so he closed the restaurant.

Later, in 1899, Mr. Abiko and four friends bought two Japanese language newspapers and combined them, naming the new paper *Nichi Bei Jiji* (Japanese American Times). This newspaper was important to the Japanese who had recently arrived from Japan. They did not know how to read English yet, so a newspaper in Japanese gave them both the news from Japan and the news in America. Besides covering news, the *Nichi Bei Times* gave advice to readers on American customs.

The immigrants needed to learn American customs. Table manners in Japan and America were quite different. For example, Japanese ate with chopsticks only, not forks, knives, and spoons. They considered it good table manners to pick up a soup bowl, lift it, and drink out of it as they had done in Japan. Americans did not pick up a soup bowl and drink out of it. So when a Japanese picked up a soup bowl in an American home, he was quite embarrassed to find that it was considered to be very bad manners. Other customs, too, were different, and the *Nichi Bei Times* advised the Japanese to learn American customs to avoid embarrassment.

Through his newspaper, Mr. Abiko encouraged Japanese to stay in America rather than returning to Japan. Most of the Japanese immigrants were men, and many of these men had come to America with the idea of "getting rich fast" and returning to Japan. Mr. Abiko told the Japanese what a good place America was and advised Japanese men to marry, raise a family, and settle in America.

Mr. Abiko even provided an answer to the problem of starting a family in America. Through his newspaper, he told the men that they should ask their parents or relatives to arrange for a wife from Japan by writing letters and sending pictures. If they returned to Japan to seek a wife, it would cost a great deal of time and money. Letter-writing and picture-exchanging meant they would only have to pay for a one-way passage for the bride. This was called the "picture bride" system. Many followed his advice and started families.

By the early 1900's white Americans began to protest against the Japanese, claiming that the Japanese were taking jobs away from them. Members of the labor unions demanded that the Japanese not be allowed to join their unions. American newspapers printed untrue stories about the Japanese. Japanese immigrants and their children began to be treated unjustly in many ways.

In October of 1906 the San Francisco School Board for the second time passed a resolution putting all Japanese school children into a separate school. This segregated school only had other Asians—Chinese and Koreans. Mr. Abiko organized a protest against this form of discrimination.

Yes, the Japanese did protest! The resolution affected not only those older students from Japan but also Japanese children born in America. Their parents did not wish to have their children put into separate schools far away across the city. They wanted their children to have the best education possible in an integrated neighborhood school, not one that was organized according to race. This was an insult to their fine children! When the San Francisco School Board and the mayor did not listen to them, they sent a letter of protest to the Japanese ambassador in Washington, D.C. They sent a representative to Washington to deliver the letter in person.

President Theodore Roosevelt was angered by this unjust treatment of the Japanese. It was embarrassing to the United States Government, which had been trying very hard to establish good relations with Japan. The mayor of San Francisco argued that it was a local matter; it did not concern the federal government. President Roosevelt stated firmly that if a local matter threatened friendly relations between two nations, then it was a concern of the United States Government. So, the San Francisco School Board was forced to return the Japanese children to their neighborhood schools. It was Mr. Abiko's strong leadership that led to this successful result.

In 1909 Mr. Abiko returned to Japan to visit Niigata, the place where he was born. He had not been there for thirty years since running away from home. In Tokyo during his visit, he met a woman named Yona Tsuda Suto. Yona and Kyutaro were married and returned to America together to continue working for the Japanese people.

After the San Francisco school segregation issue was settled, the United States and Japan negotiated and signed a Gentlemen's Agreement in which Japan reluctantly agreed to stop allowing Japanese laborers to go to America. Again Mr. Abiko protested this unfair agreement, but his protests fell on deaf ears. Mr. Abiko next set out to create in California a place where Japanese people could settle and live without fear of unjust treatment. He, therefore, organized the Central California Land Company. The company purchased a large area of land in Livingston in the San Joaquin Valley. Livingston was almost desert-like and his friends laughed at him for wasting money so foolishly on such barren land.

At this time, about 1907, most of California was just plain wilderness. One could travel for miles and miles in the San Joaquin Valley and only see land which looked like desert. There were only weeds, jack rabbits, and coyotes. It was very dusty whenever the wind blew. In the summer the area got very hot and dry. Most people thought of the San Joaquin Valley as a useless wasteland.

Mr. Abiko set out to tell the Japanese people of his dream of a place where all people would live and work together. He dreamed of a community of Japanese who would settle in Livingston and become part of an integrated community. Many Japanese people had come in the same pioneering spirit as people from other lands and they were willing to try their hand at taming this wild desert land. By this time Mr. Abiko opened a bank which even loaned these pioneers money to start their farms. This settlement was known as the "Yamato Colony."

For years the residents of the Yamato Colony fought the dust, the hot weather, and the weeds. Coyotes came to eat their chickens and skunks came to eat the eggs. After trying many kinds of crops, the settlers found the things that grew best were peaches, almonds, nectarines, and grapes of all kinds. Their thriving orchards yielded abundant crops.

Although people in other communities were treating the Japanese and their American-born children unjustly, the people in Livingston and the surrounding communities welcomed the Japanese. They invited the Japanese to join Boy Scout troops, churches, and other organizations. Nisei children attended the public schools and joined sports and musical groups.

Eventually the *Nichi Bei Times* added the first English section for the English-speaking children of the Japanese immigrants. This section helped the Nisei learn about what Nisei in other parts of the state were doing. It even had a small comic section which followed the daily adventures of Etta Kett. Through Etta's experiences, many lessons in etiquette were taught. For many years the *Nichi Bei Times* enjoyed the largest circulation among all the Japanese language newspapers.

The lifetime mission of Kyutaro Abiko was to help the Japanese and other Americans to understand each other fully and to live together in true democratic harmony. Kyutaro Abiko came to America with a dream for his people and spent his life making his dream come true.

Agricultural Kings

GEORGE SHIMA—THE POTATO KING

"There's an old saying that a lioness pushes her cubs off a cliff
to test their strength and agility. The cubs that find a way back
to her, she cares for. The ones that don't make it back,
she abandons. I feel that I am one of those cubs,
at this point in time, and I intend to make it back.
I am returning to the island. Those of you that want to
come with me, please come. And those who will not
be returning with me, I wish you well."

So spoke George Shima with determination after he and his workers were flooded off a Delta island.

The Delta in California is a hauntingly beautiful patchwork of islands and tracts. They are quilted together by channels and sloughs and pulsated by the Sacramento and San Joaquin rivers. The flatlands made rich farmland because they were created by the accumulation of mineral-laden sediments combined with reeds and tules that had rotted and matted for thousands of years to produce layers of peat. This peat averages some eighteen feet in depth. Toward the west, the peat is about fifty feet deep, and toward the northern edge it shallows to four feet. When this fertile peat was first discovered by some unknown settler, the on-going struggle of holding the water back from the swampland began.

Since the 1850's, the Delta has been reclaimed through the construction of dikes, dams, and levees. Thus, it has been transformed into 300,000 acres of the the richest agricultural land in the world. There are times when high spring tides from the Pacific combine with strong winds and rolling river runoffs to submerge the islands. Then sections of this cropland is given back to swampland.

It was just after one of these compulsive combinations of nature's whims when George Shima gave his talk about the cubs. He had just lost his home, all his farm equipment, and the farmland he had worked so hard to reclaim. If he was frustrated, he did not dwell upon it. He focused on thenext issue.

George Shima was born in 1864 as Kinji Ushijima in Kurume City, Fukuoka, Japan. His family had been farmers for generations. Kinji became interested in Chinese classics at an early age. His view of life was strongly influenced by the teachings of Confucius. Confucius was a Chinese philosopher who emphasized devotion to parents, family and friends, and the maintenance of justice and peace. He became skilled at expressing his thoughts in a style of Chinese poetry.

Kinji left his home in Kurume to go to Tokyo to continue studying Chinese classics. When he sought to enter the present Hitotsubashi University, he failed the entrance examination because of his limited knowledge of English. This failure made him decide to go to the United States to learn English. First he returned to Kurume to obtain the consent of his parents. His mother agreed to help finance his trip. He arrived in California in 1888 when he was 24 years old.

After working in various American homes as a houseboy, he went to New Hope, California to work as a laborer for a farmer, Arthur Thornton. He cared for Mr.Thornton's orchards. He was allowed to plant potatoes and onions on about three acres in among the rows of fruit trees on a share-the-crop basis. The harvest was so bountiful that Kinji Ushijima was on his way to becoming what some called the "Potato King of the San Joaquin Delta'while others tagged him as "California's Potato King' as early as 1906.

Early in his career he chose the name George Shima to simplify it and make it easier to sign his name. After that he was known mainly by his English name.

From the initial three acres of share-cropping with Mr. Thornton, George Shima moved on to farm ten acres. Then it was 25 acres. He eventually cornered the potato market in the Delta. But before he became successful, he had many years when he barely earned enough to pay back what he owed others. He lost money more often than he gained it. His daughter remembered her father saying, "Every 10 years I hit it big, but people think every year is big." But his steadfastness paid off. He began to make profits, big ones.

In 1909, George purchased a handsome three-story house with a big yard in Berkeley, California. Citizens of this university town, including a college professor cried out in protest. They did not want a Japanese family in this all-white neighborhood. When they confronted him, George said, "Don't worry, I'll build a

George Shima's house on the corner of College Ave. and Parker in Berkeley, California.
Courtesy T. Inouye

high fence to keep your children from playing with mine." He built a big high fence and stayed!

The acreage he farmed increased to cover twenty-four islands and tracts exceeding hundreds of thousands of acres, some of which he owned and some of which he leased. Along with potato growing, he also held stock in a firm founded by local investors. It was a development company called the California Delta Farms Company. The firm developed about a dozen islands and tracts, including the Shima tract named after George Shima.

The development or reclamation of swamp land consisted of building a high wall or embankment around a swampy islet so that the river would not flow into it. At first the consistency of the soil was like mud pie. Then a wide ditch was dug across the islet so that leftover water could drain and settle in it. This extra water was pumped back into the river by an engine or sometimes by siphoning. After a period of drying, the land was cleared by burning the reeds and tules. The land was then plowed and left unplanted for one to two years so that small plants and other debris could rot in the soil. George experimented to see which crop would grow best in this ground. He found that the land was excellent for growing potatoes. Marsh which had been of no value became one of the richest farmlands in the world.

Some of the farmers became jealous and fearful because George Shima happened to be Japanese. George and others like him were buying farmland and producing bigger crops. The Japanese numbered only two percent of the population of California, but produced ten percent of the crops. Feelings against the Japanese became so intense that finally in 1913 the Alien Land Law was passed. This law stated that "no aliens ineligible for citizenship shall own land." Of all the immigrants that came to the United States, only Asians were declared ineligible for citizenship. George Shima worked hard against these discriminitory policies.

In 1908 the Japanese Association of America was organized to protect the rights and security of Japanese living in the United States. George Shima was elected its first president, holding that office until his death. He sacrificed much of his time and money fighting discrimination.

George Shima also formed the Empire Navigation Company to manage his holdings, including the many vessels he ran and his large produce business dealing in potatoes, onions, asparagus, and other Delta products.

His potatoes were in such high demand that his two potato crops each year were sold while they were still in the ground. After harvest, gunnysack-loads were hauled to the river landings where George Shima's own fleet of towboats, barges, and gasoline launches transported them to wholesale buyers in San Francisco, Sacramento, and Stockton.

A wheelhouse from one of his vessels is preserved and exhibited at the National Maritime Museum in San Francisco. The description on the historic ships tour-sheet reads:

> "To your left is the wheelhouse of a much smaller river tug—50 feet in length—built in Stockton, California in 1912. She was named after a successful Japanese potato farmer and businessman who was instrumental in building the delta dikes and farmlands. He became known as the 'Potato King of the San Joaquin Delta.' "

George Shima was not only the Delta's first potato grower on a grand scale, and a wholesaler, but he was the first shipper to adopt a trademark. Packed in red sacks they were labeled "Shima Fancy." These were known to be of superior quality. The potatoes were carefully washed and graded before sacking. In this way, he pioneered in setting product standards, now known as quality control, where produce is sorted according to quality.

By 1920, he was the undisputed leader of potato growers. He was described as "far and away the most successful Japanese in California", by Manchester Boddy. He had over 500 employees from all ethnic backgrounds. The United States House Committee on Immigration in one of Shima's launches sped through the winding San Joaquin waterways to view the delta lands which Shima developed. The Committee was very surprised to view Shima's vast achievements.

If there was one big disappointment in George Shima's life, it was the passage of the Oriental Exclusion Act in 1924 which prevented further Japanese immigration. George Shima felt victimized after decades of fighting discrimination

The wheelhouse of George Shima's river tug at Hyde Street Pier. *Courtesy T. Endo.*

with all the resources he had. This included writing to and personally approaching people in politics and high offices of government.

It was two years later while on a business trip to Los Angeles he suffered a stroke and died at age 62. He left his wife, Shimeko, a daughter, Taye, and two sons, Togo and Rindge. On the day he died, he was awarded the Fourth Ranking Rising Sun Medal from the Emperor of Japan. The Associated Press headlined: "George Shima, California's Potato King, Dies in South." By this time his estate was estimated at $15 million. To illustrate his fame, both David Starr Jordon, chancellor of Stanford University and James Rolph, Jr., Mayor of San Francisco were amongst the pallbearers at his funeral.

George Shima is known and remembered for his agricultural achievements. Stockton, from where his lifetime operation took place, keeps his memory alive with a Shima Center at the San Joaquin Delta College. At its dedication in 1975, George Shima was remembered not only for his contribution to the farm economy, but also for helping a number of young people to attend Stanford University and the University of California. He is also remembered for his political activities on behalf of all Japanese Americans. A bronze plaque on the outside wall of Shima Center contains the following words:

A pile of Shima's potatoes. *Courtesy T. Inouye*

Sacks of potatoes ready for shipping. *Courtesy T. Inouye*

SHIMA CENTER
San Joaquin Delta College
Dedicated May 3, 1975
Named for George Shima
1863-1826
Agronomist, Agricultural Innovator, Philanthropist, and Reclaimer of Delta Land.
He developed sorting, grading, and mass marketing of the potato and kindred crops.

The Shima Center fittingly houses instruction in agriculture and natural resources, broadcast, fine arts, home economics, business and photography. The photography department is one of the largest West of the Mississippi River. In addition there is the Shima Gallery which provides artistic displays.

George Shima's long-time friends described him as a man of strong will, for without it how could he have continued to study Chinese classics and yet manage large-scale farming? He was a man of charitable kindness or why would he have helped the poor without racial discrimination or sent a vesselful of relief items to his mother country when she suffered serious disasters?

George Shima had another side, too. Unknown to most, he was also a poet. The Chinese classics had remained his spiritual support, and he had continued to write poetry in the Chinese style. His pen name was "Betten" meaning "another world" or "a different world."

A published volume of his literary work is titled "A Collection of Betten's Poems." In it there are fifteen poems dedicated to his former teachers: seven poems mourning the often mentioned birds and flowers and their relationship to man. One of his poems loosely translated reads:

Plum Tree in the Snow

An anti-Japanese group inflicts persecution on us on one side
My business goes wrong on the other side
Many hardships come upon me one after another
But I am in high spirits
I never yield to anyone or to anything
As a plum tree branch never breaks even under the snow.

Because of his enthusiasm for study, he received great responses from many of his teachers and solid, continuing relationships were formed which existed until their deaths. Whenever George Shima had a reunion with a former teacher or a long-time friend, he would quickly tear a sheet or two from his pocket-book and write a poem to present and to receive critical comment.

How can one not admire a man who was strong enough to tame the Delta and yet have such a soft spot in his heart as to write poetry? It is easy to say, "We love you, Mr. Shima, and we thank you for the heritage you left us."

Agricultural Kings

KEISABURO KODA—THE RICE KING

"You can't hit a home-run if you don't keep swinging," Keisaburo Koda used to say as he placed one fist over the other and made short swings at phantom balls. His friends in California heard these words whenever they urged him to stop seeking a new business venture after failing in a previous one.

"You can't let a strike-out get you down," he would assert. And he must have said these words often, for he made and lost many fortunes before settling down in a remote town about 60 miles northwest of Fresno, California in a place called South Dos Palos, where he eventually became known as the legendary "Rice King." Born in 1882 and raised in Ogawa, a small village in Fukushima in northern Japan, he probably never heard of Horatio Alger, but he did hear of Andrew Carnegie and John Rockefeller. Their stories eventually influenced him to leave a secure and respected position as principal of a village school to emigrate to the United States.

His father was a samurai, considered an expert in using the long-handled spear-like sword called the naginata. When his warrior days were cut short by Japan's shift toward becoming a modern nation, he became a successful rice miller. So Keisaburo was never really poor, the usual reason for people to leave one's homeland to seek a better life in another country.

When Keisaburo was about sixteen years old, he became a guide to a man from Tokyo who came to Ogawa to hunt fox. From this man he heard about America and about the vast resources there. Keisaburo listened so intently to his stories that when the fox hunter returned to Tokyo, he sent Keisaburo a book containing biographies of the ten most successful men in America. Among the stories were the biographies of Carnegie and Rockefeller. After reading these, Keisaburo was never quite satisfied living in his small village. America became like a magnet to him.

In 1906 Keisaburo came to San Francisco to join his younger brother, Sakae, who had preceded him to America. Together, the two brothers moved south to San Jose to work in the onion and strawberry fields. They became a part of the migrating workers, laborers who follow maturing crops. The two went up and down the state of California working at everything they could find, stooping in lush fields, toiling in the sun and rain, sleeping in shanties—and all for meager pay. They soon realized that the value of a person seemed to be measured by how quickly one could fill a container with fruit or vegetables. They longed to settle in one place, but it was difficult to escape from migrant work.

From the beginning, Keisaburo showed a flair for business. Whether he was qualified or not, he always asked for the foreman's job. When he went to pick apples in Watsonville, he made a deal with the owner. He would be allowed to pick up the discards and use them in any manner he chose. So, Keisaburo awoke very early in the mornings before the others were up, to collect the rejects. In the evenings he did the same thing after all the workers had left. He sold these apples to the local fruit dryer and made some extra money.

After the apple harvest, he went to Castroville to work in the sugar beet fields, then to Salinas to dig potatoes. During slack periods, he went to Monterey to work in a laundry. He once went to the Coalinga area to drill for oil. Failing in that, he went to work in a hotel for $50 per month. After he had saved some money, he started a laundry. Then he opened a second laundry. These he followed with yet another laundry in Palo Alto.

Not satisfied with the laundry business, Keisaburo headed for Southern California. He heard that fishing was a profitable business in San Pedro for the Japanese. He went there only to discover that although the fishing was good, marketing of the catch was not. Together with the Tajima brothers of San Pedro, Keisaburo started a wholesale fish company. In order to raise capital he went back to the San Francisco area looking for investors.

During the trip seeking sponsors, he talked with Rikizo Takata of Oakland, who urged him to grow rice, instead. "If you have any money at all, put it into growing rice...not fish," Mr. Takata recommended. He referred to a man named Mr. Nishihara who was successfully growing rice in Texas. "Japanese have been growing rice in Texas since 1902," Mr. Takata continued. "California is ten years behind. Japanese pioneer rice growers are making money in Texas...lots of it!"

Keisaburo stuck to the fishing business and it grew. The wholesale fish market boomed during World War I and his investors received a good return on their money. But the boom was short-lived. With the end of the war, competition increased. The supply of fish began to dwindle. Anti-Japanese sentiments began to spread. The future outlook seemed rather dim and his facilities needed improvement. Fortunately, about that time, a man named Nelson Kettle came along and offered to buy this business for $250,000. It was a considerable sum of money for that time, so the company was sold.

In 1917 Keisaburo married Yoshie Kawashima, a petite woman who was working for the *Nichi Bei Times*, a Japanese language newspaper published in San Francisco. She was described by one writer as a "well-educated, polite, and open person." The couple moved to Los Angeles. They operated the Golden West Produce business and sold it a year later.

In the meantime, Keisaburo had not forgotten what his friend, Mr. Takata, had told him about rice growing. With his wife's encouragement, he decided to try it. The couple moved to the Sacramento area and began growing rice on 1400 acres on a share-cropping basis. The Kodas took all the business risks and paid all expenses, including labor and materials, while the landowner received 50 percent of the gross income free and clear.

The Kodas realized that they would never get ahead as sharecroppers, so they decided to go it alone. Keisaburo rented 1000 acres in Sutter County to grow rice. A friend wanted to join him, so another 800 acres were rented. The 1800 acres were planted in early 1920. But when the crop was almost ready for harvesting, a flock of migrating geese descended upon the fields and began devouring the grain. No matter how hard the farmers tried to scare off the geese, it was to no avail. Most of the grain was lost. What little was left was destroyed by an early downpour. This one-two punch left the Kodas and their friend with a $140,000 loss.

When Keisaburo's friends from Southern California heard of his plight, they came to see him and urged him to give up and go south again to work in the produce market. But he refused. He had entered the race to grow rice and he was not about to give up. "Life is a relentless tug between the ideal and reality, and a farmer can't let the whims of nature whip him," he maintained and he stood fast.

Many years later, Shuichi Sasaki's memoirs described Keisaburo in the following way: "In spite of his sturdy, imposing frame, he had gentle eyes that reminded me of an elephant. He was a tall, moustached gentleman. His independence and perserverance stemmed from his hereditary background, a long line of warrior ancestors. He was not the type of person to settle for anything less than what he set out to do."

In Chico, California, a Mr. Miyamoto owned and operated the Chico Union Rice Co. The Kodas went there to work as laborers. The following year they rented 1000 acres to grow rice. This time they made a profit. Then a Jewish friend gave the Kodas financial backing to grow 2000 acres of rice in Woodland. This effort was a success and the Kodas finally overcame their financial woes.

During the years 1924 to 1927, he entered into several rice growing projects in Yolo county and was able to make profits of $20,000 to $30,000 yearly. But because he was an alien, ineligible for citizenship, he learned that he couldn't even rent land now. The anti-Japanese mood had gotten worse. "I will not be kept landless," Keisaburo vowed as he went on searching for a way to get land.

About that time, he heard that the great land baron, Henry Miller, was selling off some of his vast holdings in the San Joaquin valley. Keisaburo went to see it, liked what he saw, and proceded to form the State Farming Co., Inc. with his American-born childen as stockholders. His corporation negotiated to buy 8000 acres in Dos Palos at $45 per acre for a total cost of $360,000 to be paid off in ten years.

For a time everything went well. Keisaburo experimented and successfully produced better and better quality and yields of rice. His success increased the value of the surrounding land. His profits soared.

He pioneered the planting of rice from low flying airplanes. Other rice growers followed his example. His neighbors also began spraying insecticides on their orchards and fields by plane. And in the tiny town Dos Palos, where the population then was around 1,000, an airplane company was born. Ten to twelve planes were kept at all times, including two that belonged to the Kodas. By 1932, Keisaburo was growing more than 10,000 acres of diversified farm crops including rice. His fields stretched out for miles.

Always working under the threat of an early rain, Keisaburo experimented with rice dryers. He designed and built his own mill. His business continued to flourish. The Kokuho brand — meaning country's treasure — of rice was born. He bought more land, leased more land and raised rice and sweet rice — a glutinous form of grain used to make rice crackers and rice flour. He also raised cotton, lettuce, cantaloupe, barley, garlic and livestock. Keisaburo's estimated worth was more than several million dollars.

When World War II broke out on December 7, 1941, Keisaburo was immediately subjected to vigorous interrogations over long periods of time by the FBI. When the townspeople heard of this, they quickly came to his aid by vouching for his integrity and loyalty. They also pointed to the many contributions he had made for the benefit of the community. Finally the FBI, not finding a shred of evidence disproving such vouchers, relented and allowed him to be removed from California with his family. He first was sent to the Merced Assembly Center and then to the Amache Relocation Center in Colorado.

Keisaburo Koda in a rice field with the harvester. *Courtesy E. Koda.*

Son Edward Koda loading sacks of rice for shipment. *Courtesy E. Koda.*

When the war ended, Keisaburo returned to his farm to discover that two-thirds of his land and the mill had been sold without his knowledge. In addition, he did not receive any payment. One thousand hogs had mysteriously "died." His mechanized farming equipment had vanished. In just three short years, he lost most of what had taken him 34 years to accumulate. Although he outwardly appeared unaffected, a close friend wrote that "he suffered great emotional stress." He felt betrayed by people he trusted. But disciplined by a lifetime of determination and persistence, he drew strength from within to begin over again. "The secret to success is to keep trying," he told himself as he started to rebuild.

Keisaburo was now 63 years old. But this time he had his sons, William and Edward, to help him rebuild. And rebuild they did. The remaining land they controlled became known as the Bill & Ed Koda farm. The brothers developed and marketed a new rice, the Kokuho Rose. It became an instant success and was soon universally known for its high quality that surpassed the old Kokuho rice.

Keisaburo tried his hand at art too. He designed the logos which still remain the trademarks of the Kokuho Rose brand of rice and the Shochikubai sweet rice.

Despite all the success Keisaburo was to reap during his lifetime, he was beset with personal tragedies. He was preceded in death by his widowed daughter, Florence, who died at age 31, leaving a ten-year-old son. Then in 1956, his eldest son, William, died at the age of 43, leaving a wife and two daughters.

Eventually Keisaburo and his wife who had toiled by his side for so long, retired to a home in San Francisco. In his retirement, he became more public-spirited than ever. Now he had time for expanding his idealism and spirituality. He turned his energies to fighting for the welfare of Japanese Americans.

He helped form an insurance company that would give full coverage to the Japanese during a time when most insurance companies were reluctant to have them as clients.

He persuaded the Bank of Tokyo to open a branch in California so the Japanese could readily go for loans, without fear of discrimination. He worked tirelessly in the struggle to gain citizenship rights for the Issei. He encouraged young Japanese nationals to come to visit America to study different agricultural methods and to promote better understanding between Japan and America. These were but a few of the many services he performed.

In 1964 Keisaburo Koda died while visiting Japan with his wife. He was 82 years old. He received numerous citations and awards including the Order of the Sacred Treasure, Third Class, from the Emperor of Japan. He was cited for promoting better understanding between Japan and the United States and for serving as a role model for other immigrants. In San Francisco, his funeral was co-sponsored by several groups including the Japanese American Citizens League,

The Ed Koda family, l-r. Robin, Ross, Mrs. Tama, Mr. Ed and Laura. *Courtesy E. Koda*

the *Nichi Bei Times,* the Bank of Tokyo of California, and the International Farmers Aid Association.

The company that Keisaburo founded was to undergo yet another name change, this time to Koda Farms, Inc. Their products can be found in most Asian stores as well as supermarkets such as Safeway. In the May 22, 1985 issue of the San Francisco Chronicle, food writer Bruce Cost wrote the following: "Glutinous rice is available in all Asian grocery stores. Koda Farms packages a rice of fine quality."

Unlike many family businesses where the children go on to pursue other fields, Keisaburo's son, Edward, still owns Koda Farms, Inc. His son, Ross, has also taken a strong interest in farming. In all eventuality, Keisaburo Koda's descendants wil carry on the dreams that began decades ago in a remote Japanese village with some biographical sketches of men in America. This is a good reminder that words are mightier than the sword, that they can truly inspire the human spirit to work for a better world.

Agricultural Kings

KIYOSHI HIRASAKI—THE GARLIC KING

Each summer, as cars speed along U.S. Highway 101 in California, riders often encounter waffs of a garlicky smell as they come near Gilroy. It is the "sweet smell of success" to a town, some 30 miles south of San Jose, where garlic is king. Gilroy and its nearby agricultural areas at one time produced or processed 90 percent of the garlic grown in the United States. In addition, the area processes imported garlic. These activities have led Gilroy to be proclaimed the "Garlic Capital of the World."

Each July since 1979, garlic, an unimportant-looking bulb of the lily family, is honored with a three-day Garlic Festival. The open-air marketplace at the oak and eucalyptus shaded Christmas Hill Park in Gilroy is a scene described by various newspapers and magazines as "The Ultimate in Summer Food Fair" and "The Bulb's Biggest Booster Since King Tut."

At the festival the garlic comes in all forms—fresh, dried, powdered, chipped, braided, capsuled or as pills, and even as jewelry. Recipes and books about its delightful history as food and medicine are popular items.

But how many know or have heard of the Japanese "Garlic King" who added to Gilroy's fame? How many are aware that a Japanese house, standing in the middle of what was once a productive garlic farm, is now designated an Historic Site?

Kiyoshi Hirasaki, born in 1900, came to California and eventually became known as the "Garlic King." He built and lived in the Japanese house that still stands today.

Kiyoshi was 14 years old when he arrived in 1914 to join his father and older brother in Milpitas, California. After attending school for a few years, he went to work for a farmer in Gilroy, who affectionately named him "Jimmy" and taught him about the vegetable seed business. As a result, Jimmy began growing onion and carrot seeds at a very early age.

By the time he was 21 years old, he had saved enough money to return to his former home in Kumamoto, Japan to marry a neighbor, Haruye Yonemitsu. The marriage had been arranged by both parents when Kiyoshi and Haruye were very young children. This was a fairly common practice in those days.

The groom brought his bride to Gilroy, California, and eventually the couple raised three sons and five daughters. In the early 1920's the Hirasakis bought land in Gilroy near Pacheco Pass. George Clausen, Sr., an associate of Gentry Foods, a company that processed garlic and onions, approached Kiyoshi and said, "Jimmy, why don't you grow garlic?"

"But I only know how to grow seeds," Jimmy replied, "I don't know anything about growing garlic."

"Yes, I know. And you are a good seed producer. That's why you'll be a good garlic grower too," Clausen assured him. "There's a big market for garlic. Why not try growing a little?" he insisted. Because of his continued encouragement and prodding, Jimmy began growing garlic. He became very successful at it.

In 1938 and 1939 there was a World's Fair on Treasure Island in San Francisco Bay. After the fair closed, Jimmy bought parts of the Japanese pavilion and other related artifacts. He moved these to his garlic farm. With the help of six Japanese carpenters living in the San Jose area, he used these parts to build a Japanese house. The same landscape architect who had designed and built the Japanese garden at the fair came along to create a garden.

Meanwhile, the farm prospered. Jimmy bought and leased more land, growing some 1500 acres of garlic. By 1941 he was considered the biggest garlic producer in the state.

The Japanese house was connected to the Hirasaki family home and they moved into the newly finished house in October of 1941. Two months after Jimmy and his family moved into their beautiful new home, World War II broke out. Japan became an enemy nation.

At the onset of the war, Jimmy was immediately picked up by the FBI for incarceration. The remainder of the family, his wife and eight children, boarded up their newly-finished home and sadly moved voluntarily far inland to Grand Junction, Colorado. There they decided to wait out the war since they were not allowed to remain in California.

Mr. Yoneji of Palo Alto, California had this to say about his friend, Hirasaki:

"When we were imprisoned in North Dakota, a call came for volunteer workers
to harvest sugar beets. All the able-bodied young men on the outside
had been drafted for military service and there was a labor shortage.
Of course, most of the imprisoned men rebelled. 'Why should we go out to help
harvest crops?' they argued. 'We haven't done anything wrong
and yet here we are. . .locked up. If our government can't trust us
on the outside, then why should they trust us only to go and
top sugar beets?" they angrily asked.
"But then Hirasaki said, 'Why not? We're just sitting here doing nothing. We
might as well work. Let's not sit here and rot.' With these words, Hirasaki changed
the mood of the angry group, and all those that were physically able to work
went out to harvest sugar beets, a back-breaking, dreary job."

After the war the Hirasakis returned to their former home to put their lives,
family, and farm together again. Even while he was putting his own affairs back
in order, Jimmy gave a big helping hand to other farmers who returned to the
area. He extended them credit whenever possible. He offered the use of parts of
his land for share-cropping until each farmer could buy his own land. Some
families were guests of the Hirasakis because housing was difficult to find. They
stayed with them until proper homes could be found.

In 1948 Jimmy, together with other concerned Japanese Americans, helped to
finance a new Northern California Japanese English daily newspaper in San
Francisco called the *Hokubei Mainichi*. This newspaper continues to serve as an
important way for Japanese Americans to keep in touch with the many events
within the wider Japanese American community. Jimmy served as the first
President of the Board of Directors of the newspaper. He held that position until
his death.

Jimmy built a shipping warehouse near 10th and Alexander Streets in Gilroy
in 1948. Here, fresh produce from his farms, packed in ice, was shipped to
midwestern and eastern markets in refrigerated train cars. The specialty in those
days was celery boxed under the label "Jimmy's Choice." The celery was of such
good quality that it was in great demand. Hirasaki Farms prospered once again.

In the early 1950's Jimmy moved part of his house to land near his
warehouse and donated the building and the land to form a Japanese
Community Hall. The loss of the first Community Hall during World War II had
been a bitter blow since this was the only place where the Japanese American
community could hold all its gatherings.

Before the war, scores of whole families, including young children, had
labored long and hard on weekends to plant vegetables to raise funds for the
original land and building. So many families were working together that
passersby often stopped to ask what they were doing. They found it difficult to
believe that so many people would be working without pay to support a
Community Hall.

Mr. and Mrs. Hirasaki in front of their home. *Courtesy E. Nakamura.*

Kiyoshi Hirasaki at his desk at Hirasaki Farms Packing Shed
in Gilroy, California, 1950. *Courtesy E. Nakamura.*

During the war the Community Hall was sold by the State of California
because Japanese were not allowed to remain to take care of the property and
pay the taxes. The new owner was the Grange, a powerful white farmers'
organization, which had fought for the removal of the Japanese farmers when the
war began.

Kiyoshi Hirasaki took a great interest in community affairs thorughout his life.
He was an active supporter of many causes. People with ideas came to him for
his support, and, if he found the idea reasonable and worthy, he would assist in
providing initial funds. He was known within the Buddhist Churches of America
for his long years of service.

Kiyoshi "Jimmy" Hirasaki died in 1963. The Japanese house he had built still
stands and is now occupied by his eldest daughter.

Now you know that it was a young, adventurous boy from Japan who was
influential in making Gilroy the "Garlic Capital of the World." As the *Baltimore
Evening Sun* worte, "If you are wild about garlic, visit Gilroy." And if you are
history minded, look up the Japanese house where the first "Garlic King" lived
and worked and served his fellow man.

MY WORLD OF FLOWERS
BY YOSHIMI SHIBATA

When I was a child, Father used to take me into the greenhouse and say, "Let's talk to the roses." He would say, "A rose is a living thing and it is trying to tell you something in its own language." I thought it strange, for I could never hear the roses say anything, but then, Father was always talking in riddles. Having been educated in Japan, Father had a philosophy which had a subtle and indirect impact on others.

As I gained more knowledge about the art of growing roses, I found myself telling my nursery managers to "listen' to the roses, too. I told them to observe the "body language' of the roses because these flowers are constantly revealing how happy or unhappy they are with the temperature, light, soil, humidity, air movement, and the amount of daylight. This is shown by the size and color of the leaves and flowers. When the plants are happy, an abundance of beautiful long-stemmed roses is the reward.

My interest in roses and in the world of flowers was instilled in me early in life by my parents. Father would say, "If you become a doctor, you will make your money from sick people. If you become a lawyer, your profit will come from people in trouble. If you go into the flower business, you will earn your living by making people happy."

Father's deep interest in growing flowers and starting a nursery business developed during his days as a "school boy." He was one of the early Japanese

Jenjuro Shibata, Yoshimi's father, established Mt. Eden Nursery.
Courtesy Y. Shibata.

immigrants who went to California and worked his way through school by doing house and garden work in exchange for room and board.

At first, with no money and a language handicap, Father took odd jobs. In 1906, when he had saved enough money, he started a small nursery in East Oakland. Thus, I was born into the nursery business. As a small child, I thought that all flower growers were Japanese because Father's friends were all flowers growers. My parents spent long hours at work and so I grew up believing that everyone worked long hours.

The day started at 2:00 a.m., as Father prepared to go to the early morning market in San Francisco. He packed the flowers in the "kori" (trunk-like baskets) and carted the kori by wheel-barrow to the electric train bound for the Oakland pier. For the privilege of putting the baskets in the aisle, a bouquet of flowers was given in appreciation to the conductor. This agreement between the conductor and the Japanese flower growers was made without the use of spoken language. The train ride ended at the Oakland pier, and the growers carried the baskets on board the ferry to cross the Bay. When the boat landed in San Francisco, everyone strapped the baskets of flowers on their backs and trudged to the Fifth Street Flower Market. The wear and tear on their coats from the chafing of the straps and baskets made the grower's appearance unique.

In time Father's business outgrew the nursery in Oakland. Father moved to a new property in nearby Mt. Eden and started another nursery. At the first rain part of the land was flooded and appeared useless. Instead of being upset, he simply said, "It's great. We'll make it into a water reservoir and pump from it."

Since there was no other way to go from Mt. Eden to the San Fransisco market, a Model T Ford was purchased. Self-starters were non-existent then, and cranking the engine to start a stiff motor on a cold morning more often than not resulted in blisters. The procedure was made easier by putting hot charcoal into a bucket to warm up the motor from the bottom, making cranking easier. I will never forget riding to the market on the Model T Ford at 2:00 a.m. with Father singing loudly in Japanese amid the flutter of side curtains in the windowless car.

Crossing the San Francisco Bay on a ferry meant hot chocolate and donuts. The adults chatted endlessly in Japanese about market conditions. Upon berthing at the San Francisco Ferry Terminal, Father drove off the ramp to the Fifth Street Flower Market.

Here, the Japanese flower growers rented an old wooden garage and assigned tables to each seller. From 4:00 a.m. the growers were kept very busy putting up orders for their customers before the market opened. Many retail florists had gathered at the entrance by 6:00 a.m. At the ringing of a bell, the gate was opened and the buyers turned the place into a beehive of activity. The immigrant Japanese negotiated with buyers by flashing their fingers. It was truly amazing how they managed to communicate. Father could easily pick out those who would pay a good price and those who were miserly. I learned how to analyze the business of the day by noting the number of buyers and the quantity of flowers brought there by the growers.

Competition was keen, and haggling over prices meant the difference between going home with a profit or a loss. Language was a handicap for Father, but he learned quickly how to count money in English. More often than not, growers did not make a good profit even with all the hard work. There was no time for tears—things happened too quickly to allow time for contemplation. By 8:00 a.m. it was all over and we realized a day's work was already done. The rest of the city was just beginning a new day.

The market was more than a place to sell flowers; it was a place where the growers shared ideas and experiences. The pulse of social, economic, and political activity could be felt there. The excitement and fellowship at the market became a way of life. After the selling was over, breakfast was anything from hamburgers to a bowl of noodles.

After breakfast, nursery supplies were purchased and deliveries were made. By the time we returned home, it was late morning. Mother had started the chores, such as cutting flowers and watering the plants. She did anything required of her even becoming head painter when we were building a greenhouse. Operating the nursery was a family business which included every member of the family to the youngest child.

After supper, there was "yo-nabe" (work done at night). Chores that could be done in the evening were considered a wasteful use of daylight hours. Bunching flowers was a regular night-time ritual.

Another project was building greenhouses for the precious plants. Undaunted by their lack of building skills and language to learn the skills, they improvised in the best way they knew how. Even today, after fifty years, many of these greenhouses are still in use.

One day a sudden tragic accident changed the course of our family. My older brother who was six years old was hit on the head by a rock thrown by a neighborhood boy. In spite of our best efforts, he died.

All of the family's property was in the name of my older brother who was an American born citizen. This was because the California Alien Land Law prohibited Japanese immigrants from owning property. Now Father was about to lose his property and business as he was not able to transfer the property to his other American born children. He decided to fight for his right to keep what he had painstakingly built up for his family.

Father engaged the services of a very capable attorney named Guy C. Calden. Mr. Calden was the legal counsel for the Japanese flower market and had fought numerous battles in behalf of the Japanese. The fight was for the right to form a

Mt. Eden Nursery main plant, 1950. *Courtesy Y. Shibata.*

Shibata family. Sitting, L to R: Mr. Shibata, Mrs. Shibata, daughter Yayoi.
Standing: sons Yoshiye, Yoshimi, Yoshikuni, and Yoshito. *Courtesy Y. Shibata.*

corporation of his remaining citizen children for the purpose of transfering the property and retaining Mr. Calden as the trustee until the children became of age.

Mr. Calden and Father fought the case all the way to the California Supreme Court. A landmark decision was granted in Father's favor, and he was able to continue his hard won business. Father often said that somehow, somewhere, someplace, there is a road to justice within the American system. He said the democratic process is not for the weak; a person must fight for his rights. I will never forget his intensity in fighting against such great odds. This was not a time when Japanese immigrants won many court cases.

Father's philosophy was full of common sense. It helped me through the dark days of World War II and the evacuation. Immediately after the Pearl Harbor attack, the gas company turned off our gas supply, saying it was against the law to trade with enemy aliens. It was heartbreaking to see the Christmas crop of roses freeze because fuel for heating the greenhouses was cut off.

Then came the forced evacuation. Early in 1942, the United States Army ordered us to leave our home and nursery within a short period and move far away. I was constantly running from the home, to the nursery, and the business district. I seemed on the verge of a nervous breakdown. Father tried to lift me out of my depression by saying, "Whether you run or walk, the rice paddy will still get muddy. The world is at war, and nations are being wiped out. Why are you so worried? The family is healthy and alive. We will build again. This is not the end. It's just a bad storm. Get out of the weather."

Despite the chaos of those months, mutual trust between men somehow survived. I'll always remember Mr. Gilbert, a self-made man whose lumber business prospered along with the Japanese flower growers. Father could not fully pay up his lumber bill because of the evacuation, and he wanted to assure Mr. Gilbert that he would keep his commitments. Mr. Gilbert responded by saying, "Mr. Shibata, when you come back, we will talk about it. Don't be away too long." That was the end of the conversation.

Many Japanese left the relocation camps and worked for flower growers in other states. I was one of them. During those years, I developed a broader knowledge of the industry and a better understanding of the flower industry nationally. From all the moving during the evacuation, I learned that mobility could be turned into a blessing instead of a curse. Later, my changed attitude enabled me to move anywhere in California to seek the best climate, land, and water for growing flowers.

The evacuation made me more determined to pursue the only profession I really knew — flower growing. I took solace from the serenity of flowers and sought refuge from the turmoils of the postwar world in the company of flowers.

I wanted to devote my efforts to the creation of beauty for everyone to enjoy. I had grown weary of the war and the hatred that had led to the incarceration of

Yoshimi amongst flowers

my family and others like us. The War and Evacuation were the result of a lack of effective communication between the Japanese and Americans.

I enjoy being a flower grower; for I know somehow, somewhere, my work would make someone a little happier. I know that flowers will convey those feelings which can not always be expressed well in words. The popular phrase, "Say it with Flowers," had been coined for this very reason.

I grew up in a world of flowers. I have lived in this world all my life. For me there was no better way in which I could provide for my family. I could also help people communicate more easily through growing beautiful flowers. I would not trade it for any other business in the world because everyone from the grower to the seller to the buyer has one goal in common—to make people happy!

MIKE MASAOKA
A VIGOROUS FIGHTER FOR BETTER AMERICANS
IN A GREATER AMERICA

Mike Masaoka is one of the best known leaders among Japanese Americans. He was a brave and bold leader of the Nisei during the dark days of World War II when the United States was at war with Japan. Americans of Japanese ancestry, citizens and non-citizens alike, were put in the uncomfortable position of being loyal American citizens but having faces that looked like the enemy. Over 110,000 of these persons of Japanese ancestry were ordered from their homes and put into concentration camps. Mike Masaoka was among the leaders who fought to find a way out of this tragic situation.

Mike Masaru Masaoka was born on October 15, 1915, in Fresno, California. He was the fourth child of Eijiro and Haruye Masaoka. His father had come from Japan in 1903 to seek a better life in America. Haruye came two years later and married Eijiro in 1908.

When Mike was one and a half years old, the family moved to Salt Lake City, Utah. Mr. Masaoka opened a fish and vegetable market there. When Mike was seven years old, he would go with his father to sell fish to the Japanese laborers and farmers in the countryside. While his father stayed by the truck and sold some fresh fish, Mike walked up and down the rows of houses calling out "Sakana!", meaning "fresh fish." At other times he stood in front of the family's fruit stand wearing an apron that had been folded over many times and tied so it would not drag on the ground. This seven-year-old boy would call out the specials of the day at the top of his lungs, "Strawberries, 2 cups for 19 cents!"

When Mike was only nine years old, his father was tragically killed in an automobile accident. After that, Mrs. Masaoka and the older children worked hard to keep the family of eight children together. When there was time, Mike enjoyed playing marbles, hide and seek, cops and robbers, baseball, and touch football. He also bicycled and roller skated.

After his father died, Mike's grandmother came from Fresno to care for the younger children. She lovingly shared her knowledge of Japanese customs and culture. The children learned, therefore, to appreciate things Japanese. She taught them origami, the art of folding and cutting paper to make animals and flowers. From the older boys, Mike learned judo. He attended Japanese school daily for an hour after regular school was over. As a Boy Scout, he rode on the Japanese float in a Memorial Day Parade. It was decorated with cherry blossoms by Japanese people in the community and carried pretty Nisei girls in colorful kimonos.

At home he ate Japanese meals prepared by his mother and grandmother. The family celebrated Christmas in the traditional American way. They celebrated New Year's Day, an important Japanese holiday, with special rice cakes and a bountiful feast of special Japanese foods.

When Mike went on to high school and college, he excelled in speaking and debating — he won many awards in debating contests. He wanted people to know how much he loved America. He wanted people to understand that, although his appearance was Japanese, America was his country. Mike enjoyed speaking and debating so much that he accepted a position to teach Speech at the University of Utah.

It was during this time that he began to hear more and more about the Nisei who lived in California, Oregon, and Washington, where most Japanese Americans lived. Mike discovered that the Nisei everywhere felt as he did— unhappy about being victims of racism.

The Nisei went to college to receive degrees in teaching, business, and engineering. When they finished college, they were not able to find the kind of jobs for which they were trained. They were not hired because they were Japanese. They needed to work, so the Nisei took jobs as store clerks, farmers, and fruit stand operators instead of teachers, bookkeepers, and engineers as they were prepared to be.

This unfair treatment came from many sources. Politicians circulated untrue stories that made people fear the Nisei. Newspapers printed biased stories about Japanese Americans too.

The Nisei on the West Coast began to organize themselves into a group called the Japanese American Citizens League (JACL). The JACL gave the Nisei a chance

Mike presenting a plan. *JACP collection.*

to tell America about themselves. It also gave them a way to fight together to counter prejudices and injustices against them.

While Mike was teaching at the University of Utah, he learned about the West Coast JACL and its campaign for fair treatment. He wanted to join the struggle. He went to the 1938 JACL convention in Los Angeles to share his ideas about new ways to achieve their goals. He suggested two ways:

> 1) That the JACL become a nationwide organization instead of being only a West Coast organization. He felt that Nisei throughout the country would want to become a part of this organization.
>
> 2) That the JACL be opened to anyone who wanted to help end discrimination against Japanese Americans. The JACL should not be limited to Japanese Americans. It should be open to anyone who wanted to join in their effort to erase anti-Japanese racism.

The officers rejected both suggestions. They were very unsure of this outspoken young Nisei who suddenly came into their midst.

Mike returned to Utah undiscouraged and still determined to show the JACL officers that his plan would work. He began by increasing JACL membership in his area. He invited Nisei in Utah, Idaho, and Oregon to join the organization. Mike became an officer of his JACL chapter. When he went to the next JACL convention, he was able to show how membership had increased because of the same needs in other regions. He had demonstrated how the organization could be made more effective with a broader membership.

In 1936 the Masaoka family moved to Los Angeles. During that time, the military leaders of Japan were becoming very powerful, and they were using that power to take over lands near Japan. They were already at war with China and were also making threats to other countries. America strongly objected to those actions and refused to send materials to Japan that might be used for war. Other actions brought worsened relations between Japan and the United States.

Under those international tensions, people in the United States began to confuse the Japanese in Japan with Japanese Americans. They began to question the loyalty of Japanese Americans to the American Government. The Nisei tried to convince people that they should have no reason to question their loyalty to the United States.

It was during this trying period that Mike was chosen as the first paid executive secretary of the JACL. Mike left his job at the University of Utah in September, 1941, to spend all of his time working for Japanese Americans.

He wrote a creed which told how Nisei pledged to support the United States Constitution and to defend her against all enemies. This creed has been used by the JACL ever since.

After Japan bombed Pearl Harbor in Hawaii on December 7, 1941, the United States plunged into World War II against Japan, Germany, and Italy. Japanese

Americans were shocked and fearful because their parents, the Issei, were now considered enemy aliens.

On that fateful day, Mike was in North Platte, Nebraska. He had gone there to encourage Nisei to organize a JACL chapter. He urged them to join other Nisei in campaigning against racism.

When the North Platte police learned that Mike Masaoka was a leader of Japanese Americans, they jailed him immediately. The police did not tell Mike why he was being jailed. All they knew was that he was a leader of Japanese Americans and that America was at war with Japan.

For three days no one could find a way to convince the police that Mike was not a dangerous person. Finally, the JACL was able to reach one of Mike's friends, United States Senator E.D. Thomas. Senator Thomas convinced the police in North Platte that Mike was a loyal American citizen and should be released.

People in the United States were led by false and fear-filled newspaper and radio reports to believe that Japanese Americans might help Japan in the war. Early the next year, the United States Army ordered all persons of Japanese ancestry in the West Coast states put behind barbed wire in concentration camps. Under armed guard, Mike's brothers, sisters, and widowed mother were taken to a camp far away from the coast to a desert spot called Manzanar in mid-eastern California.

Mike was on special assignment for the government, so he was able to travel because the Japanese Americans in the eastern part of United States were not sent into the camps. He spoke wherever people would gather to listen. He told them the truth about Japanese Americans; that they were trustworthy and loyal to the United States.

Several times he was put in jail by local police who took him for a spy. Once, Mike went to New Orleans, Louisiana to speak before a national social workers' conference. He and his Nisei friend, George Inagaki, went sightseeing in George's car just as you might do the first time you visit a city.

At that time the people of New Orleans were fearful because of a rumor that a German U-boat had been sighted and spies had entered the city. A deputy sheriff arrested Mike and George, convinced they must be the spies, as Japan and Germany were allies. He refused to believe in their innocence, and even put them in separate cells.

When Mike did not appear for his speech, the program chairman of the Conference began to search for him. She called the F.B.I. and asked them to help find Mike and George. The F.B.I. finally found them in the jail and rescued them.

Mike traveled on to Washington, D.C. to help Japanese Americans who were still in the ten concentration camps scattered throughout the country. He called on government officials, members of Congress, and religious leaders to tell them about the people in the camps.

Mike receiving Legion of Merit from General Wood at Leghorn, Italy, 1945
Courtesy M. Masaoka

He pointed out that Japanese Americans had been denied their basic rights as law-abiding citizens and residents of the United States. They had been imprisoned without any specific charges being brought against them and without proof of any wrong-doing. Mike asked that these innocent people be released and allowed to help America fight the war. Furthermore, he asked that young Nisei men, who were in the camps, be allowed to help fight in the war instead of being imprisoned.

When the United States Army was convinced that the Nisei could help in the war, they asked the Nisei in the camps and in Hawaii to volunteer for duty. The Army was suprised when they received more volunteers than they had expected.

The volunteers formed the 100th Battalion and the 442nd Regimental Combat Team. They fought valiantly in Europe against the German and Italian armies.

The motto for these Nisei soldiers was "Go for Broke," Hawaiian slang for "Give it everything you've got!" These men were out to prove once and for all that no one should have any doubts about the loyalty of Japanese Americans. They were outstanding in their single-minded will to accomplish each job assigned to them. They lived up to their motto through unselfish sacrifices for the benefit of all Japanese Americans, most of all for their loved ones behind barbed wires in concentration camps in the United States.

The 442nd Regimental Combat Team was the most decorated unit in the history of the United States Army. Mike, himself, received the Distinguished Service Cross for his valor.

President Truman conferred the Presidential Unit Citation on the Regiment and said,

> "You fought for the free nations of the world... You fought
> not only the enemy, you fought prejudice—and you won!
> Keep up that fight—continue to win. Make this great Republic
> stand for what the Constitution says it stands for,
> 'the welfare of all the people, all the time.'"

After the war, the fight was not yet over for Mike and Japanese Americans. It was time to do something about correcting the many unjust laws which discriminated against their Issei parents. These discriminatory laws had been passed because white people feared competition from the Japanese in America.

After World War II, Mike Masaoka, leading the Japanese Americans, mounted an all-out campaign to correct those unjust laws. First he helped to obtain some payment for the losses suffered by the 110,000 people of Japanese ancestry when they were forcibly removed from their homes, farms, and businesses. He helped to secure passage of the Evacuation Claims Act in 1948, which paid a small percentage of the losses—ten cents for every dollar lost.

In 1952, after intense lobbying by Mike and the JACL, a law was passed which allowed the Issei to become naturalized citizens. Large groups of elderly

Japanese, including many who had been in America for over forty years, flocked to the naturalization offices to apply for citizenship.

In 1965 Mike's efforts led to the passage of a law which now allows people from Asia to emigrate to the United States on the same basis as people from Europe. This law has made possible increased immigration from China, Japan, Korea, the Philippines, and South East Asia. It erased the Immigration Act of 1924, commonly called the Exclusion Act, which had stopped Japanese from immigrating to the United States for 41 long years.

Today, Mike maintains an office in Washington, D.C. and continues to work on behalf of Asians and all minority groups, particularly in fighting for civil rights. He very ably represents Japanese Americans in their efforts to secure legislation for redress of wrongs suffered by them during evacuation and internment in World War II. The efforts emphasize acknowledgement by the United States Government that a wrongful deprivation of human and civil rights occurred at that time and that restitution must be made in the interest of justice.

He is ever watchful of developments in United States-Japan trade relations. Mike has the special skill to be understood by both Japan and America as an American. He is respected by both nations for his ability to communicate to both nations.

In war and in peace Mike has led the way for Nisei and their Sansei children to continue the fight to establish "liberty and justice for all."

DANIEL K. INOUYE
FIRST JAPANESE AMERICAN CONGRESSMAN

"Raise your right hand and repeat after me," announced the Speaker of the U.S. House of Representatives.

The gallery of the United States House of Representatives was hushed. All were aware of this historic moment. The first Congressman from the new state of Hawaii was about to take his oath of office. It was August 23, 1959. The great hall grew still quieter as Daniel Ken Inouye raised his left hand, not his right. He had no right hand; it had been lost in battle while Dan was a young American soldier during World War II.

Daniel Ken Inouye—U.S. Congressman! Election to this high office was far beyond the wildest dream Dan could have had as a boy. He grew up in a poor and crowded neighborhood on Queen Emma Street in Honolulu, Hawaii. He was born on September 7, 1924. Almost directly across the street stood the Pacific Club where rich haole (white) gentlemen and ladies gathered. Asians could not become members.

Dan's grandparents, poor farmers from Japan, had come to Hawaii in 1899 to work on the ever-growing Hawaiian sugar plantation. The ten dollars a day they earned seemed like immense wages to hard-working immigrants. They were part of the great wave of Asians who arrived in Hawaii from China, then Japan, the

Philippines, and other parts of the Far East from 1850 on. So great was the demand for Asian workers on the growing sugar cane fields that by 1900 three out of every four people in Hawaii were Asian.

Dan was Japanese and used chopsticks to eat with, but he also liked hamburgers, and used spoons and forks. Like many other Japanese Americans, he had never lived in Japan.

Dan enjoyed every moment of his childhood. In his innocence he once asked his mother if he would ever be able to marry the daughter of the Emperor of Japan. Thinking long and seriously, his mother replied with the words that would influence Dan for the rest of his life.

"No one is too good for you," she paused, then continued, "but remember—you are no better than anyone else, either."

Dan was not to forget these words as he worked with people from all walks of life and of all skin colors in later life.

Dan's belief in equality was tested in a painful experience during high school. Most of his schoolmates at McKinley High School were of Japanese ancestry from poor neighborhoods. He was a good student and was assigned to the top tenth grade class in which the students wore white shirts and polished shoes. These students had adopted the more formal dress and behavior of the haoles as a sign of their superior achievement in school. Dan continued to go to school in a sports shirt and denim pants, like most of his friends.

That same year in the tenth grade, Dan's teacher recommended him for membership in two honor societies. His parents were proud. Before Dan could become a member, however, he had to pass an interview. In the interview he faced four older students who asked, "Why should you be in an honor society? You don't even wear a white shirt or a tie. And what kind of friends do you have? They're delinquents!"

Dan tried to answer, but he was interrupted. He lost his patience over the last remark. Angrily, he shouted, "My friends are not delinquents, no more than I am or you are! Do you call them that because they're poor? I thought you were going to ask me about my interests and ideas, about my schoolwork. But if you're just looking for guys who wear white shirts and shoes, you don't want me." Dan started to leave, then turned and added slowly, "And I don't want you!"

Dan Inouye was angry, and he resolved to prove to the interview team that shoes and neckties were not what really mattered. He was not willing to copy their way of dressing just to join the honor societies. This strong determination to recognize performance and achievements would appear again and again later in his life when Dan was faced with challenges.

In high school Dan studied hard in his desire to become a doctor. He passed a Red Cross First Aid course and began teaching his own classes. His high

Bombing of Pearl Harbor December 7, 1941.
Dan hurried to help with the wounded. *U.S. Navy.*

school years were quite normal for a seventeen-year-old. His life was suddenly changed one Sunday in December of 1941.

On December 7, 1941, Japanese war planes attacked Pearl Harbor, bombing American naval ships in port and damaging American aircraft. Dan was getting ready for breakfast and for church afterwards when he flicked on the radio and was stunned by the news, "This in no test! Pearl Harbor is being bombed by the Japanese."

Outside his home Dan could see black puffs of smoke in the direction of Pearl Harbor. He felt grief and shame all at once. Anger against the army of Japan welled up within him and he kept saying to himself, "Why did they do it? Why couldn't they let us live in peace?"

For five days Dan worked at the first aid station, caring for the injured and the dead, and helping dazed people search for missing loved ones. No matter how hard he worked, he had to endure the insults of those who called him a "dirty Jap."

Now Dan's life revolved around the defense effort, working at night as a medical aide from 6:00 p.m. to 6:00 a.m., attending morning classes at high school, and catching what little rest he could in the afternoon. At seventeen years of age Dan was assuming the responsibilities of a man.

The Japanese Americans in Hawaii tried to show that they were loyal Americans. They bought more bonds than any other group in Hawaii. Older men offered to help in any way they could, even collecting garbage and digging ditches. College students strung up barbed wire along the shores and guarded beaches against possible enemy attacks.

Soon after the attack on Pearl Harbor, about 1,500 Japanese in Hawaii were ordered to leave their homes and were imprisoned without a trial. They were considered by the American Government to be dangerous enemy aliens and were whisked away to prison camps in the continental United States. And they were separated from their families for months and months.

The following spring, Dan decided to enter *Scholastic Magazine's* national writing contest, which was open to all interested students. He had a story to tell. He wanted to tell about December 7 and about how it felt to be an American-born citizen with a Japanese face helping the injured and dead of Hawaii. He wanted to bare his feelings of shock and anger.

Dan's story won first prize in all of Hawaii. It went on to compete at the national level and earned honorable mention. Dan's story appeared in the summer issue of *Scholastic*. Dan had won one of Hawaii's highest honors.

Now the high school honor society invited Dan to become a member. He remembered the humiliation he had suffered when he was first asked to join. He carefully considered the invitation. He decided to set aside the hurt and humiliation he had suffered, and accepted it.

It was not until a year after Pearl Harbor that Japanese Americans were allowed to join the American armed forces and fight for their country. Anxious to prove their loyalty on the battlefield, more than 10,000 Japanese American men volunteered for service. This was about eighty percent of all qualified Japanese American males of military age.

Dan was part of the large group of young Japanese American men in Hawaii who stormed the draft board to enlist. He was only eighteen years old. At the time of his discharge from the United States Army, he was a Captain in an all-Japanese American unit.

The unit that Dan belonged to was called the 442nd Rigimental Combat Team. This unit was composed almost entirely of Japanese American men. Their motto was "Go for broke!", meaning "give it all you've got." The men lived up to their motto and established the following extraordinary combat record:

Named the most decorated outfit in the U.S. Army.
Won ten unit citations.
Honored with 3,915 individual decorations,
including 47 Distinguished Service Crosses
and a Congressional Medal of Honor.
Lost about 700 men on the battlefields.
Suffered a high rate of injuries because of their bravery.

Daniel Inouye as a soldier of the 442nd Regimental Combat Team.
Courtesy Go For Broke, Inc.

Dan, himself, lost his right arm in combat. Despite this loss, he made up his mind that there was not a thing in the world he couldn't do with his left hand if he wanted to do it badly enough. He had survived the bloody war and was going back to his home.

Dan and each member of the 442nd received a hero's welcome. His parents were quietly proud that their son had added honor to their family name and had offered his life to his country at a time when the loyalty of Japanese Americans was being questioned.

Dan began to realize, however, that another hard battle had to be fought at home. Prejudice against Japanese Americans was ever present. On his way home to Hawaii after V-E Day, he stepped into a barber shop in San Francisco for a haircut. He was dressed in his captain's uniform with the insignia of the U.S. Army. One sleeve was empty of the arm that had been severed in combat. The barber refused to serve him saying, "You're a Jap. We don't cut Jap hair."

Once again, Dan felt the crushing hand of blind prejudice. He thought to himself, "We ought to have every single right that every other American has. Why is this denied us?"

Dan continually looked for ways to gain equal treatment for Japanese Americans. How could he fight this second battle of helping to "make a world where every man is a free man, and the equal of his neighbor"?

Dan decided that government would be the best place he could help bring about changes. He thought that the people of Hawaii, too, were ready for changes. In 1954 he ran for office and was elected to the Hawaiian House of Respresentatives. He became the majority leader. When Hawaii was accepted into statehood in 1959, he became the first Representative to Congress from the State of Hawaii. In 1962 the people of Hawaii sent him back to Congress, this time as the first American of Japanese ancestry elected to the United States Senate. Since that time, he has won every reelection to the Senate and continues to serve on congressional committees as a member, counsel, or chairperson.

Throughout his life, by example and by deed, Daniel Ken Inouye has tried to live by the principles he believes in, the ideals of "equality and justice for all" upon which our nation was founded. His life story conveys the true spirit of the words, "I am an American!"

YOSHIKO UCHIDA
AUTHOR OF CHILDREN'S BOOKS

Yoshiko Uchida was ten years old when she wrote her first stories in small booklets she made from brown wrapping paper, and she has been writing ever since. On the day she graduated from elementary school she began a "Journal of Important Events" in which she recorded all the special events of her young life—the happy times, as well as the sad.

"By putting these special happenings into words and writing them down," she says, "I was trying to hold onto and somehow preserve the magic of those moments. And I guess that's really what books and writing are all about."

When Yoshiko was growing up, there were no books about Japanese Americans for her to read, and she knew of no Asian American writers. She had no professional role models, so she never dreamed that one day she would become a writer, providing today's children with the kinds of books she lacked in her own youth. Today she is the first full-time professional Nisei writer of books for young people.

She has now published twenty-four books and several short stories for young people, as well as many articles and one book for adults. She has also written a yet to be published novel for adults and has received more than twenty honors and awards of excellence in writing.

A writer performs the difficult task of putting ideas and thoughts down on paper. We can all have vivid thoughts and scenes in our minds, but it is quite another matter to communicate them in written words. It is not easy. But Yoshiko has achieved just that, and now she has a large following of readers who, through her books, can feel and understand the world that is hers.

Yoshiko was born in Alameda, California, and grew up in Berkeley during a time when being a Japanese American was not easy. "I always felt that I was different and not quite as good as white Americans," she explains. "I grew up having to ask such questions as, "Will the neighbors object if we move in next door?" or "Can we come swim in your pool?" And when I went to a beauty parlor for my first professional haircut, I called first to ask, "Do you cut Japanese hair?"

But if she felt rejected by society, she and her older sister were surrounded by love and warmth at home. Their parents also instilled in them the richness of Japanese culture, values, traditions and beliefs.

Yoshiko grew up in a home surrounded by books, where the written word (both Japanese and English) was important. Her mother, who perhaps was more of a role model for her than anyone else, read many Japanese stories and books to Yoshiko and her sister. Her mother was also a poet, who wrote many beautiful tanka, the thirty-one syllable Japanese poem.

Both her parents were great letter writers and kept in touch with many friends in Japan. As a result, the family mailbox was always bulging and their home constantly filled with visitors from Japan. At the time, the visitors seemed dull and boring to Yoshiko, but now that she is a writer, they often provide wonderful material for her writings. There was one perspiring visitor, for instance, who excused himself in the middle of a holiday dinner to remove his heavy winter underwear because he was so warm. When he returned to the table with a big grin, explaining what he'd done, Yoshiko and her sister had to rush into the kitchen where they burst into laughter. Many years later, the gentleman appeared in one of Yoshiko's short stories entitled, "Excuse Me, I Feel Much Better."

"Our life experiences are always with us," Yoshiko says, and she often draws from the memories of her past. She finds bits and pieces of her child-self turning up in her writing, especially in her three books, *A Jar of Dreams, The Best Bad Thing,*, and *The Happiest Ending*. These books are not about her own family, but they focus on a young Nisei child, Rinko, who also grew up in Berkeley during the depression years and often felt as Yoshiko did in her youth.

Yoshiko attended the University of California at Berkeley, where she earned a BA, with honors, in English, History and Philosophy. But before she could receive her diploma, Japan dropped its bombs on Pearl Harbor and her peaceful life was suddenly shattered.

Yoshiko,(2nd right) age 10 with parents, grandmother and older sister(far right).
Courtesy Y. Uchida

Along with thousands of Japanese Americans, she and her family were uprooted from their home in Berkeley and interned first at Tanforan and then in the Topaz, Utah, concentration camp, one of ten such camps in which 110,000 Japanese Americans of the West Coast were interned.

While in camp, Yoshiko taught in the elementary schools, and also took teacher training classes where her interest in children's literature first developed. Although she still had no thought of becoming a writer then, her instincts as a recorder caused her to keep a diary that later helped her write the book for adults, *Desert Exile: The Uprooting of a Japanese American Family*, which told of her family's wartime experiences.

Yoshiko also turned her wartime adversities into book successes with the publication of *Journey to Topaz* and *Journey Home* written for young people.

Whenever she speaks to children at schools about these books, she always asks them why they think she wrote the two JOURNEY books.

"To tell about the camps?" they ask. "To tell how you felt?" But eventually they come up with the right answer. "You wrote them so it won't happen again," they say. And she makes sure the children understand that freedom is our most precious possession.

After almost a year in camp, Yoshiko was able to leave Topaz to attend Smith College in Massachusetts on a full graduate fellowship. She earned a Masters degree in Education, taught school in Philadelphia for one year and eventually moved to New York City.

In New York, she published her first book, *The Dancing Kettle*, a collection of those Japanese folk tales that she heard and loved as a child, and was embarked on her writing career. Yoshiko began with folk tales because she loved their universality and she hoped that by sharing each other's stories, Japanese and American children could eventually share ideas as adults.

In 1952 Yoshiko spent two years in Japan on a Ford Foundation Fellowship. While there she collected more folk tales and also became interested in Japan's folk art and crafts which were the subject of many of her later articles. "Most important, however," she says, "I became aware of a new dimension to myself as a Japanese American and deepened my respect and admiration for the culture that made my parents what they were."

In her earlier books, Yoshiko wrote primarily of the children of Japan, hoping to erase the stereotypic image many non-Asians held of the Japanese people and to portray them as human beings.

As young Sansei began to seek their identity and sense of self, however, Yoshiko wanted to reinforce their self-knowledge and pride. "I also wanted ALL young people to have a sense of continuity and a feeling of kinship with the past," she says.

She changed her focus then to writing about the Japanese experience in America. She wrote such books as *Samurai of Gold Hill*, which told of the first settlers from Japan—the Wakamatsu Colony. She also wrote picture books about young Japanese Americans, *The Birthday Visitor* and *The Rooster Who Understood Japanese*. And, of course, there were the books about her wartime uprooting.

In all these books Yoshiko has evoked a strong sense of the strength and courage of the Issei, who endured and survived so many hardships. They were strong and had a sense of hope and purpose in life. They displayed the kind of spirit which Yoshiko hopes today's young people will cherish as well.

Although all her books have been about Japanese people, Yoshiko says, "We must be proud of our special heritage, and it's also important to remember that we must understand not only ourselves, but *all* people. Together, we must celebrate being human beings."

Yoshiko Uchida is known primarily for her writing, but because of her writings she has spoken to more than 4000 children about her experiences as a Japanese American and as a writer. She has been interviewed on TV, radio and in many publications. Her books are widely reviewed and recommended.

It is interesting to realize how her family's love for the printed word and for all kinds of people influenced Yoshiko. Countless numbers of people have become devoted readers of her writings. They are blessed by being able to share her world of thoughts and experiences.

EDISON UNO
FIGHTER FOR JUSTICE

Edison Tomimaro Uno was a man of vision whose dreams for the future went far beyond those of most people of his time. He shared his dreams with many people and therefore his dreams live on in the minds of those he influenced with his kind, gentle humor and iron-willed determination.

Edison was the ninth of ten children born to George Kumemaro and Riki Uno of Los Angeles. He was born on October 19, 1929.

Edison was twelve years old when World War II began. That sad and fateful seventh day of December, 1941, marked the beginning of his life-long quest for justice and equality for all Americans.

The attack on Pearl Harbor by the Japanese navy changed overnight the lives of Japanese Americans. The United States went to war with Japan, the home of their ancestors. All persons of Japanese ancestry, even small children and U.S. citizens were suspected as being enemy agents. They became fearful and anxious because of the strong hatred expressed against them on the radio and in the newspapers.

In February, 1942, two months after the outbreak of war, the Uno family felt the full force of the hysteria and fear among the general public and within government circles. One afternoon, two men from the FBI appeared at the door of their home, showed their badges and asked for Edison's father.

The friendly manner of the FBI agents impressed young Edison, but it hid their true purpose—to issue an arrest warrant to Mr. Uno and to take him down to FBI headquarters for questioning. Edison innocently thought that this must be a routine check of all Japanese heads of households by the government. His father had done nothing wrong and had never been previously arrested.

After a long, anxious wait, a call finally came from the FBI informing the family that Mr. Uno would need pajamas and toilet articles. The family suddenly realized that the arrest was for more than routine questioning. They now understood that their father was not only going to be detained, but held for deportation as a dangerous enemy alien without benefit of legal procedures.

Along with thousands of other non-citizen Japanese, Mr. Uno was to experience imprisonment in distant freezing-cold camps in the middle of winter. These camps were in areas such as Missoula, Montana, and Fort Lincoln in Bismark, North Dakota. Other camps that Mr. Uno was transferred to included the Prisoner of War camps at Lordsburg, New Mexico, and Santa Fe, New Mexico.

Mr. Uno was not allowed to contact his anxious family for almost a year. Edison, along with his family, was very confused by his father's status as a prisoner of war when he was not guilty of any crime.

"Surely," thought Edison, "this has to be a mistake. Father is not an enemy of the United States. He is as patriotic as any American. It was he who had taught us all about loyalty to America."

In the meantime, the family was ordered to evacuate from their comfortable home in Los Angeles to the crude and crowded make-shift living quarters in the Santa Anita Race Park. They were later moved to Amache Relocation Center at Granada, Colorado, in the middle of a hot and dusty desert. They, too, were being moved about secretly by the United States government just as Mr. Uno was.

The family was finally reunited at a special detention camp in Crystal City, Texas. There, Edison came into contact with several hundred Japanese families that had been deported from Peru in South America and were waiting to be sent to Japan. They spoke Spanish rather than English. Undaunted by the language barrier, Edison organized useful activities for the young people.

After the war ended, the Uno family, with the exception of Mr. Uno, was released and allowed to return to Los Angeles. Edison refused to leave without his father. Reluctantly, the rest of the family left Crystal City.

Edison stubbornly remained with his father until Halloween Day of 1946. He was finally persuaded to return to Los Angeles to continue his education.

Years after his internment experience, Edison was fond of saying that

Young Edison with his father in Crystal City, Texas,
in October of 1946. *Courtesy R. Uno.*

he spent 1,647 days in an American concentration camp. This time amounted to four and a half years.

The years which Edison had spent in prison camps during World War II left a lasting impression on him. Wholesale removal of people from their homes solely on the basis of their race, both U.S. citizens and non-citizens alike, and their forced internment in concentration camps under armed guards was not what this country stood for. This was what Edison was taught to believe. Justice had failed badly!

The dreadful war-time experience caused Edison to seek justice from the United States Government for all the Japanese in America who had been imprisoned in those out- of-the-way concentration camps. He set a lifelong goal of getting the government to officially admit that it had made a mistake and to make amends for this terrible error. It was important to him to do this because he believed in American justice for all and he did not ever want to see the internment happen again to anyone.

Upon his return to Los Angeles, Edison attended John Marshall High School, where he was President of the senior class. When he was sent to a national conference of the Hi-Y, a YMCA youth group, he was again elected president. And, as President of the East Los Angeles chapter of the Japanese American Citizens League at the age of eighteen, he became the youngest chapter president of that national organization.

Edison married Rosalind Kido in Los Angeles. Soon after, he enrolled in Los Angeles State College. After graduation, he enrolled at Hastings College of Law in San Francisco, California.

Midway through law school, Edison suffered his first heart attack. He realized that his heart might not bear the strain of intensive study and of caring for his wife and a baby daughter named Elizabeth Ann. Heeding the advice of his doctor, Edison reluctantly gave up his goal of becoming a lawyer.

Although he knew his life might now be cut short at any time, Edison continued to work hard to promote justice through wise laws. He wanted to build a better world for his children. He could not "take it easy."

When his health improved, Edison did everything he could to tell people about the injustices done to the Japanese in America. Through teaching, writing, making speeches, and taking part in numerous community and civic organizations, he informed people that laws must be made that are just, and laws that are unjust must be corrected.

In 1972 many fair-minded people rejoiced when the United States Government finally removed a dangerous law, Title II of the McCarran Internal Security Act of 1950. This law had given the government permission to arrest and imprison people, if they were thought to be spies or helpers of enemy nations, without a fair trial in court.

The rejoicing became possible only because Edison and Raymond Okamura of Berkeley, California led many people and organizations in working together on a massive three year campaign to erase a bad law.

Edison sometimes did things alone when others were too timid to stand up for liberty and justice. And when he started an important project, he worked on it no matter how long it took.

For example, Edison tried for fifteen years to get an apology from former United States Supreme Court Chief Justice Earl Warren for his part in locking up Japanese Americans behind barbed wire during the war. As Attorney General of California in 1941, Mr. Warren had agreed with those who wanted to remove all the Japanese in California after the war had begun and had even suggested that they all be sent out of the country, citizens or not.

Since Mr. Warren had shown fairmindedness as Chief Justice, Edison thought it was time to seek an apology so that the historical record could be cleared. Edison wrote letters to Mr. Warren and tried to meet with him whenever Mr. Warren came to Northern California from Washington, D.C. While the apology was not made openly, Edison learned that, prior to his death, Mr. Warren had written in his memoirs that he regretted his war-time actions toward Japanese Americans.

No matter what the occasion, formal or informal, Edison usually wore a tweedy brown sportcoat over a turtle-neck sweater. He kept his wardrobe simple so that he could focus his attention on his mission in life and on his family whom he loved and to whom he devoted what little free time he had. His family had increased to two daughters with the birth of Rosann.

At times Edison's neat but casual appearance fooled people. A favorite story Edison enjoyed telling happened when he was chosen to serve on the San Francisco Grand Jury in 1970.

The Grand Jury always has many well-known civic and political leaders. On the day of the installation ceremony, Edison drove into the parking area reserved for Grand Jury members in his ten-year-old Rambler. The guard on duty, eyeing Edison's clothing and old car, tried to block his entrance into the parking lot. Edison ignored the guard and drove into a parking space between a shiny Cadillac and a luxury model Continental Mark IV.

Flushed with anger, the guard hurried over and spoke curtly to Edison. He said, "Who do you think you are? This place is reserved for members of the Grand Jury!"

Edison smiled, showed his pass and told the furious guard, "I *am* a member of the Grand Jury!"

In 1969 there was a student strike at San Francisco State University over the issue of freedom of speech and the rights of ethnic minority students. Edison took an active part in supporting the striking students. He spoke out against the

Edison with students at the College of San Mateo. *Courtesy R. Uno.*

San Francisco, California, 1976. L to R: David Ushio, National Director, JACL;
Congressman Norman Mineta; Edison; James Murakami, JACL President;
President Jimmy Carter; Don Hayashi, JACL Washington Representative;
and Mrs. Judi Ushio. *Courtesy R. Uno.*

president, Dr. S.I. Hayakawa, who later stated publicly that the government was justified in evacuating the Japanese from the West Coast during World War II.

When Iva Toguri D'Aquino, a Japanese American woman, received a presidential pardon for her alleged World War II radio broadcast from Japan as Tokyo Rose, Edison was named as one of those who had worked to get the pardon granted. That pardon was necessary because an innocent person had been forced by an enemy nation to work for them and had suffered humiliation for many long years. Today her record is clear, thanks to the steady and skillful support of concerned people like Edison.

Edison urged people to fight for their civil rights and to speak out for justice. He would say, "Write letters to your city, state, and national leaders. Call them; send them a wire. Tell them how you feel."

Michi Weglyn finished writing an important book titled *YEARS OF INFAMY, The Untold Story of America's Concentration Camps* largely because of Edison's strong encouragement and support. Edison himself helped write an elementary grade book titled *Japanese Americans: The Untold Story* in 1970.

At home Edison's desk was always piled high with mail. He often typed far into the night on his faithful typewriter. His ideas poured out from his sharp mind and turned into letters, speeches, and news articles that touched the lives of many people.

Knowing how powerful the media could be in influencing people, Edison took full advantage of opportunities to discuss the war-time evacuation of the Japanese whenever he appeared on television or radio. For, in 1942, it was the media which had hurt Japanese Americans by describing them as evil and dangerous people who would sabotage the United States.

"The media now must tell the truth about what happened in World War II," he would say. "Only then will people believe and understand the wrong done to Japanese Americans in 1942."

NBC produced *Guilty by Reason of Race*, a program which is still used in schools, colleges, and universities throughout the country. Edison was behind the idea of producing it, and he assisted with its production. This was only one of the many television productions in which he was called upon to act as advisor.

On December 24, 1976 Edison's heart finally gave way. He was 47 years old. Edison Uno lived and died as a fighter for justice. He never lost faith in America and what she stood for—the right of all citizens to life, liberty, and the pursuit of happiness!

In 1984, following a year of congressional hearings across the country, bills were introduced in the United States Congress to call attention to the Japanese American internment. These bills asked the United States Government to apologize to Japanese Americans for their treatment during World War II. The bills also asked for redress for the sufferings and losses they experienced. Edison Uno, in his quest for justice, had planted the seed for redress as early as 1972 when he began to talk to anyone who would listen about the importance of achieving justice for Japanese Americans.

Edison was a man of ideas. But he was not content to just think and ponder. When he had bold ideas he could be counted on to act boldly. Edison Tomimaro Uno was truly a man of action!

Short Stories 8

UNCLE KANDA'S BLACK CAT
BY YOSHIKO UCHIDA

UNCLE KANDA'S BLACK CAT
BY YOSHIKO UCHIDA

Whenever I see my cat sitting very still, dreaming his quiet dreams, I wonder if he is thinking of old Uncle Kanda.

He wasn't really my uncle. He was just a friend of Mama and Papa's who went to their Japanese church once in a while. I never knew exactly what he did for a living, and I didn't much care. I never talked to him unless I had to because, like all the other kids, I was sort of scared of him. He was a tall, bony man who looked as though he had always been old. His face was full of wrinkles, like crumpled up tissue paper. His hair and his shaggy eyebrows were white, and there were milky rims around the pupils of his eyes. I remember his clothes always seemed worn and wrinkled, as though he'd been wearing them for a long time.

The kids in the neighborhood said he had magic powers and could cast an evil spell on anybody he didn't like. They said he kept lizards and snakes and toads in his room and that he dried them and ground them up to make medicine that he tried to sell. Sometimes I wished I could go see his lizards and toads, and maybe he'd give me one for a pet. But on the other hand, I didn't want to risk having him cast an evil spell on me.

The reason I finally did go to see him one day was because he lived only a block away from our house in a room above an old garage on Carleton Street, and because Mama felt sorry for him.

She had made a big bowl of vegetables and vinegared rice, which I loved, and she had fixed up a plate for old Uncle Kanda. She made a small mountain of rice on a paper plate, decorated it with strips of egg and dried seaweed and red ginger, and then wrapped it up in wax paper.

"Will you take some osushi to Uncle Kanda, Rinko?" she asked. I tried saying, "Why can't Ko take it?" Ko was my little brother, and wasn't much use to anybody.

"Because he's too young," Mama answered. "You're older, Rinko. Be a good girl and go, will you?"

And so I went. I held my breath as I climbed up the creaky steps outside the shabby old garage, because Herman, who lived next door, told me that would make me invisible. I didn't believe Herman, of course, but I kept thinking how funny it would be if I really did get invisible. Then old Uncle Kanda would open the door, and there would be this plate of osushi floating in the air, with me nowhere in sight.

"He won't be able to cast a spell on you if you're invisible," Herman told me.

"Well, come with me and watch to see if it happens," I said.

But Herman shook his head. "Not me," he answered. And he wouldn't admit that he was just as scared of old Uncle Kanda as I was.

When I knocked on Uncle Kanda's door, a big black shape suddenly leaped from the roof of the garage and pounced on me with a screeching yowl. I let out a scream and dropped the osushi, and then saw that it was only Uncle Kanda's big black cat. "Scat, you dumb cat!" I said, stamping my foot. I picked up what I could of the osushi and piled it back on the plate. It had a little dirt mixed in with it now, but I explained it was all his cat's fault. Uncle Kanda sort of smiled then and said a little bit of dirt wouldn't hurt him.

One day when Mama made a sponge cake for her Ladies Aid meeting, she cut a big slice and put it on a plate. Then she asked me to take it to Uncle Kanda.

"Aw, Mama..." I was in the middle of a good mystery story and besides, I still had to do my thirty minutes of piano practice.

"Please," Mama coaxed. "You know how lonely he is."

I didn't know anything about being lonely. How could anybody be lonely? There were millions and zillions of people in the world. And millions and zillions of books to read. There were hills to hike, and movies to see, and stores uptown to go roaming around in. What was the matter with Uncle Kanda that he was always lonely?

I carried my grumbling thoughts with me as I ran to Carleston Street. I held my breath and ran up the sagging steps. Maybe, I thought, I'd just knock and leave the cake by his door and run, so I wouldn't have to talk to him.

But today the front door was slightly open, which was strange, because Uncle Kanda usually kept it bolted from the inside with two locks. His black cat sat guarding the door looking just like one of those great lions that guard the temple gates in Japan. I glared at the cat and he glared right back at me. Now I couldn't put the cake on the doorsill or the cat would eat it up.

I knocked on the door, but didn't hear the usual shuffling of Uncle Kanda's slippers. I was wondering what to do when he called out, "Rinko, is that you?"

I didn't answer. I could still run. But he called again. "Rinko, will you please come in?" He sounded as though he were talking from inside a hollow box. I pushed open the door and went in. I looked quickly around the small room. The shades were drawn so it was dark and gloomy, but I could still see what a mess it was. There were stacks and stacks of old books and magazines and newspapers scattered all over the floor. It looked like a second hand book and junk shop that no one had ever bothered to tidy up. There as a gray enameled coffee pot and a dirty cup and saucer on a table in the middle of the room. I was disappointed because I didn't see a single toad or lizard or snake, but on top of a bookcase I saw a faded brown photograph of a lady in a Japanese kimono. Beside it there was a vase with a dried up marigold that must have been there for six months. I was wondering who the lady was then Uncle Kanda called me again.

There was a screen in the far corner of the room opposite the small sink and stove, and behind it, there was Uncle Kanda lying in bed all wrapped up in a faded patchwork quilt. He didn't look as though he could cast an evil spell on anybody. He just looked tired and pale and old.

"Rinko," he said quietly. "Go home quickly and ask your mama to call Dr. Yamata for me."

I knew then that Uncle Kanda was really sick. I forgot I was still holding onto Mama's cake and ran all the way home with it. The funny thing was Uncle Kanda's black cat came with me, as though he had to make sure I'd do as I was told. After I told Mama about Uncle Kanda and she called the doctor, I gave the cat some milk and left-over toast. He crouched carefully over it, flicking his pink tongue in and out, and lapped it all up. When he finished, I gave him some more and he ate that too, as though he hadn't eaten in weeks.

Dr. Yamata fixed Uncle Kanda up with some medicine. It turned out that his heart wasn't in such good shape. But that wasn't all. Dr. Yamata came to talk to Mama and Papa afterwards, and I heard him telling them that he was just as worried about Uncle Kanda's stomach.

"His stomach?" Papa asked, puzzled.

"Yes," the doctor answered. "It is quite empty. He simply isn't getting enough to eat."

Mama was shocked. "Oh, poor Mr. Kanda," she said. "We'll see that he gets some proper food."

After that, she and Papa went to the corner grocery and bought a bag full of food. They filled Uncle Kanda's cupboard with tins of salmon and beans and condensed milk and jam. The next day was Saturday, so they both spent hours cleaning and straightening up the mess in Uncle Kanda's room, and they let in some sunshine and fresh air.

When Uncle Kanda got stronger, I was the one who had to go over almost every day. I took pots of steaming soy bean soup with cubes of tofu, or cups of hot egg custard, or slices of ham and chicken, or rice balls with pickled plums. I took whatever Mama fixed, and sometimes I'd try to make Ko go with me so I'd have some company. But he always shook his head.

"Not me he'd say, just like Herman. "I don't want old Uncle Kanda to git me."

"He's not going to git you. Don't be stupid."

But Ko wouldn't budge. He was scared of the old man, just the way I used to be.

Now that I knew Uncle Kanda was just a plain ordinary human being who didn't grind up dried lizards and toads, I even began to like him a little bit. His cat stopped pouncing on me when I went up the squeaky steps, and I stopped holding my breath and trying to be invisible.

Now that Mama and Papa had cleaned his room, there was a place for me to sit at the table beside Uncle Kanda.

"Stay a while, Rinko," he'd say. "Tell me what you've been doing."

Then I'd tell him about being in the school play, or about how I hated practicing the piano, or how I took Ko uptown to see "Tarzan" at the Saturday afternoon movies. I even told him about my new school shoes and the new dress I got for my birthday.

"Will you wear it for me someday?" he asked.

"Sure," I answered. I was suprised he was even interested in dresses.

He kept me talking all the time he ate whatever it was that Mama sent over to him. I could see how it would be more fun than eating all alone, so I stayed until he was finished, and then brought home Mama's plate or pot.

One day I asked him about the lady in the photograph. "Who is she anyway?" I wondered. "She needs a new flower whoever she is."

Uncle Kanda put down his chopsticks and looked over at the photograph as though he hadn't seen it there every single day of his life.

"That lady? Why she came over from Japan to marry me."

I was so suprised, I just sat there with my mouth open. It never in the world occurred to me that anyone would even think of marrying Uncle Kanda.

"When was that?" I asked at last.

"A long, long time ago. When I was young and strong. When I used to work for sixteen hours a day picking fruit in the valleys. When I steamed up to Alaska in the summer to work in the canneries. When I used to wash windows and scrub floors for the rich white people who lived up in the Oakland hills."

It was hard to think that far back in time or to imagine Uncle Kanda as a young man with black hair and a strong body.

"And so she came from Japan and married you?"

Uncle Kanda grew very still, as though his body and soul had drifted back to that time long ago.

"No," he said, almost in a whisper. "She died of influenza one month after she arrived, before we could be married."

I felt a chill go down my spine. It was as though the ghost of the Japanese lady had suddenly drifted into the room to tell Uncle Kanda how sorry she was that she'd never been able to marry him.

I jumped when Uncle Kanda's cat suddenly leaped into my lap with a small cry. I stroked his silky black body and rubbed under his chin and heard him begin to purr. He closed his green eyes and became a warm silky hunk of pure perfect blackness.

"Issa likes you," Uncle Kanda said. "He doesn't like most people."

"I know," I said.

It had taken him a long time to get to like me. Now Uncle Kanda told me he was named after a famous Japanese poet who wrote haiku. As I rubbed under his soft silky chin, I suddenly began to like him back. He was the first cat I ever liked, because Ko and I always had dogs. I never did have much use for cats until then.

One afternoon not long after that, when I took over some meat loaf for Uncle Kanda, he didn't answer the door. It was locked from the inside and when I knocked, I didn't hear anything except Issa's mewing on the other side of the door.

Mama looked worried when I cam home with the meat loaf. As soon as Papa came home, she went with him to see what was wrong with Uncle Kanda.

When they came back, they had brought Issa with them, and I knew something had happened to Uncle Kanda.

"Is Uncle Kanda sick again?" I asked.

Mama shook his head. "No, he's gone to heaven."

"Oh."

"But you mustn't feel too sad," Papa said. "We found a letter for you in his belongings."

Papa handed me a long thin evelope with my name on it. The writing was shaky, like a very old man's handwriting would be. The letter inside was very short.

"Dear good friend Rinko," it said. "I want to give you the one thing I love the most, my faithful cat, Issa. Please be good to him. Uncle Kanda."

So now Issa is my black cat, and when I see him sitting very still, dreaming his own small dreams, I think maybe he is remembering old Uncle Kanda. Then I think about him and remember him too, and I hope he and the lady from Japan finally did get together, someplace over there, wherever they are.

ONE HAPPY FAMILY
BY TOSHIO MORI

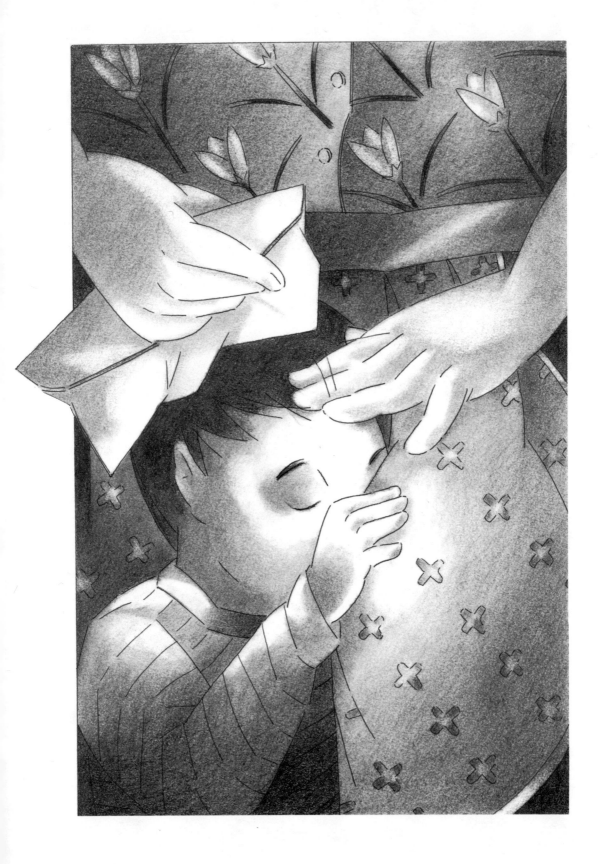

ONE HAPPY FAMILY
BY TOSHIO MORI

The postman's familiar footsteps were audible to the little American Japanese boy and his mother. It was nine in the morning. The improvised mailbox rattled and they heard the postman going away. Ben, the seven-year-old son, ran to the door but his mother was quicker. She took the letter and brought it in the house.

"Is it from Daddy?', Ben asked his mother.

The seven-year-old son stood below her as she intently read the letter. He pulled her apron when she did not answer.

"Is it from Daddy, Mama?", he asked again.

The mother looked away from the letter and then sat down. "Yes, Ben. It is from Daddy," she said quietly.

The room became silent again, and the silence of the house shook little Ben's persistence. His lips opened to say something sharp because his mother would not confide in him. He looked at the quiet figure of his mother and his resentment faded away. Yes, she was keeping something from him but she was sad. He could not be angry at her when she was so sad.

"Ben," his mother began, "your father is, I've often told you, away on a long vacation. The letter says that his trip will probably be long but it may be short too. It depends entirely on his business, Daddy says for you to be patient and be a good boy, a good, fighting American boy."

For a moment Ben's brown Japanese eyes twinkled and his face lit up. Then a frown clouded his face. "What kind of business did Daddy go on? Why did he have to go away?"

His mother did not reply. She stared at the blank wall a long while.

"Mama, did Daddy run away?" Ben asked his mother.

"No, no!" the mother replied quickly, "Daddy would never run away."

She reached for her knitting bag and began knitting a sweater that was too big for Ben and too mannish for herself. Ben watched her quick, skillful fingers move swiftly, and then he saw them gradually lose their speed until her fingers barely moved.

Suddenly he cried, "I know! He's dead! Daddy's dead!"

The mother raised her hands and gasped. "Ben! Don't say that again!"

"He's dead, Mama. He's dead."

His mother shook her head vigorously. "Ben, you must believe me. Your father is alive. He is on a vacation. You must take Mother's word for it."

"He's dead, I know," Ben said.

"No, Ben," she said quietly.

Ben faced his mother triumphantly. He knew his Dad was alive. His letter had come, hadn't it? Yet, Mama was hurt. He saw her hurt look when he made guesses about dad. He must be on the right track. All of a sudden his eyes opened wide, and he knew why his father was not home, why his mama must suffer and become sad. He remembered the headlines of the city papers, he recalled that one day when a strange group of older boys at school called him a "Jap" and chased him home. America was at war with Japan, but he could not understand. What had war to do with their home, with his quiet father who had worked hard for a living? His daddy must have done an awful thing to be sent away.

Ben heard his mother sigh and glanced up. He looked at her lost face and sighed too. "Mama, did he do something bad? Is he a bad man in America?"

His mother gave a cry so sharply that Ben sat up straight, and then he saw that her eyes were wet. He looked away, triumphant for a moment. Knowing he had found out the truth at last, he felt big and wise like a grown-up man.

His mother came over and put her arms about him. Her eyes were soft and her hand on his head was soft. "He is innocent, Daddy is. Please remember that, Ben. Don't ever be ashamed of him. Believe in him."

"Why was he taken away, Mama?" he asked.

Mother shook her head slowly. "He was taken as a suspect but he is not guilty. He was taken because America doubted him and he had no explanation. And please, Ben dear, never become bitter. America is for us plain people. Believe in America. Bitterness is not for the common man. When you grow up you will realize that this war was fought to destroy bitterness, sadness and fear."

Ben could not understand her words. He wondered if everything would turn out right. He became doubtful of ever seeing his dad. If he had a wishbone like his friend, Frankie Brown, back home he would wish for the world to turn out right. That was all he would wish for, and realizing his helplessness he buried his face in her apron and sobbed softly.

High over his head he heard the soft words, and the tender stroking of a hand. "Stop crying, Ben. He will come back when the government investigates his case. He will be back free."

The world swam before his closed eyes as he clung tightly to her skirts. The little boy continued sobbing because even a mother cannot soothe and comfort one at times.

GAMBATTE
BY VALERIE PANG

GAMBATTE
BY VALERIE PANG

The tennis tournament line judge yelled, "Out."

I knew it was match point. I clenched my jaws. "I've got to win this point," I told myself. "If my opponent wins this service, I'll lose the match."

I bent my knees and leaned foward. With my knees bent I was ready to spring wherever the ball landed. The opponent served the ball hard. It was a good serve. The ball bounced next to the center line. Just as I swung my racket to return the service, I slipped and fell to the pavement. The ball flew past me and landed inside the line. I had lost.

"Midori, are you all right?" shouted my friend, Sara, from the sidelines. Sara was my very best friend. She was also on the school tennis team.

"I'm O.K. Scaped my knees bad though," I answered.

I shook the winner's hand and limped off the court.

"Tough break," said Sara as she joined me. "The judge made some bad calls. The girl hit the ball out several times, but he didn't call them. That Jap lost the game for you."

I was stunned by what Sara had said. Had I heard right? Sara was my best friend. Why would she say such a terrible thing? I was Japanese American too. Didn't she know she had used a name that applied to me too? I was too hurt to say anything. Besides, my knees were throbbing and the blood was oozing out all over my new red and white striped tennis socks.

When Mom came to pick me up at the tournament she cried out, "Midori, what happened to you?"

I could see the alarm in her eyes and in her tone of voice. "Gee, Mom, I'm okay. Just scraped my knees. Don't worry so much. I can take care of myself."

Mom looked hurt.

"Sorry Mom," I apologized. "I've had a hard day."

"Well, let's get you home so I can clean up your knees. You get hurt more often than your brother. I told Grandma maybe you should quit tennis." Mom turned on the ignition and started the car.

"Aw, come on Mom," I pleaded. "I just fell and tripped over my own two feet. I'm fine."

At home my injuries didn't look bad. Mom rinsed off the bruises and put bandages over them. I kidded her after she wound yards and yards of bandage around my knees. "Thanks, Mom. These are great knee pads."

"O.K. you win," said Mom. "Your knees don't look so bad after all. I'm relieved."

That night as I lay in bed I couldn't help thinking about the tournament. Next time I'll win, I thought. I know I'm small and short, but I can still be a good tennis player. I can't let this defeat get me down.

As I stared up at the ceiling, I still felt depressed. Why had Sara called the line judge a "Jap"? He was a Japanese American. Didn't she know I was Japanese American too? She made it sound terrible to be Japanese. But I was just like her in many ways. I liked tennis too. I spoke English just like her. I had never thought of myself as being different from her. I felt low.

The next morning Sara and I were going to play tennis. I got up early and washed up. In the bathroom I looked myself in the eye and said, "What's wrong with me? I have two eyes, a nose, a mouth, two arms and legs like Sara. Am I so different?"

I was talking to myself when someone pounded on the door.

"Midori, hurry up. I want to use the bathroom." It was my younger brother, Pete. "Don't waste your time combing your hair and putting on makeup," he yelled. "It won't help. You are beyond help."

I got angrier by the second. I thrust the door open and almost hit his face.

As I looked outside, my anger melted away. It was a beautiful morning. The sun was shining but it was still a cool 70 degrees. The sky was a deep blue with threads of white clouds swirling against it. It was another beautiful Seattle summer day.

Someone knocked on the door. I ran and opened it. Sara stood there holding her tennis racket over her right shoulder. Her thick blond hair was tied back in a pony-tail and her big blue eyes sparkled when she smiled. All the boys in school were after her because of those lovely blue eyes.

"Hi, Midori. Ready for a good workout?" she asked.

"Sure, let's get at it," I answered. I grabbed my racket and we were out the door.

I felt better after two hours on the court. Sara didn't say anything about what had happened yesterday and neither did I. We both acted as if nothing had happened. I wasn't as uncomfortable as I was the day before, but her comments still bothered me.

"See you Monday," Sara yelled as she ran toward her house across the street. "Have fun tomorrow at your Grandma's."

I waved to Sara and went inside.

Every Sunday my mother, father, brother Pete, and I went over to Grandma Takahashi's for dinner. I usually looked forwared to going. Grandma was a great person. She was very active and was a lot of fun to be with. Sometimes we hit a few tennis balls together. She used to play tennis a lot in her younger days and she had a mean forehand.

Upon arriving at Grandma's, Pete and I dashed out of the car, trying to be the first up the porch steps. We both wanted the honor of being the first to reach the gold-colored key which stuck out from the doorbell. It was the most unusual doorbell I had ever seen. This time I was too slow. Pete grabbed the key and turned it. A small bell on the inside of the door rang, "Rrrriiiiing." I loved the sound the bell made. It reminded me of all the special times I'd had at Grandma's house. Grandma lived alone now that Grandpa Takahashi was no longer alive.

The door opened. The smiling round face of Grandma greeted us. "Well good evening, Pete. Hi, Midori. Come in, come in." She held out her arms and hugged us. No matter how old we were, she always had a hug for us. Some days I didn't like it, but this time I welcomed it.

As I went into the living room, I smelled the sweet but tangy aroma of makizushi, a Japanese delicacy made of rice, seasonal vegetables, and seafood. Grandma made makizushi for us every Saturday. Sometimes I helped her prepare the ingredients.

My job was to fan the hot rice as she poured the vinegar and sugar on it. If the rice didn't cool quickly, the grains of rice would become mushy, so speed was necessary. I was the best rice fanner around.

"Grandma, you made makizushi already. Can I have a taste?" I asked. "I'd better make sure it tastes all right before everybody else tries it."

"Sure," laughed Grandma, "but don't spoil your dinner."

While I ate one piece, Mom, Dad and Pete went out to the backyard to play with Grandma's dog, Tippy. He was the most gentle dog I had ever met. He hardly ever barked except at the mail carrier. His curly coal black fur glistened in the hot summer sun. He looked at me and wagged his tail as if he wanted me to play with him. Usually I didn't mind, but today I was just not in the mood to play. I just stayed inside.

Slumped in Grandpa's comfortable, deep chair, I heaved a big sigh.

"What's wrong, Midori?" Grandma asked. "Sick today?" She looked concerned.

"Oh nothing," I mumbled. I wasn't sure what to tell her.

"Having trouble with your forehand?" she asked.

"No, nothing like that."

"Having trouble with one of your friends?" Grandma asked as she set the table.

"How did you know?" I said in surprise. Grandma always seemed to know what was wrong.

"Well, that's part of life. I get my greatest pleasures and deepest disappointments from those close to me," she said.

I wasn't sure what to say next. All of a sudden I blurted out, "Sara called the line judge a 'Jap' the other day. That really hurt my feelings. She's supposed to be my best friend. I know she wasn't calling me a name, but she might as well have done that. I felt like she had thrown a knife into my stomach. I felt sick. I didn't know what to do. I just wanted to run away and hide someplace where no one could see me." I looked down at the maroon rug too dejected to even cry.

Grandma pulled up her silver-gray chair close to me. She leaned over and placed her hand in mine. "That's a tough problem. Even for someone as old as I am, it still hurts to hear someone call another person a 'Jap.' Since Sara is your friend, why don't you talk to her about it? She may not even know how you're feeling about it."

I could feel the burden of being Japanese getting heavier and heavier. "But why do I have to bring it up? It's her problem, not mine."

Wasn't Sara supposed to be my best friend? I was having enough trouble with tennis because I was so small and short.

Grandma must have sensed how low I was feeling. She suggested that we walk down to the nearby high school tennis court and hit some balls. She called out the window to Mom, "Be back for dinner in an hour."

As usual, Grandma brought along a huge bag of old tennis balls that she brought whenever we practiced. Grandma was my best coach. She started out by tossing the ball over the net so I could practice my ground strokes.

Feeling better I yelled, "Thanks, Grandma. Come on, let's rally."

Grandma fielded balls from one corner to the next. Then she hit a lot of lobs. I ran behind the baseline and wound up. To my own amazement I was able to hit a bullet of a return. It was great fun.

As the sun started to fall, Grandma said, "Midori, thanks for the exercise. We'd better get back for dinner. Your mom will get angry if we're late."

"Gee, Grandma you're great! Thanks for the practice. How did you know I wanted to work on lobs?" I felt very excited because I had never hit lobs so well before. Returnig lobs was usually the weakest part of my game.

"Oh, just a hunch," Grandma replied. "Remember I used to play a lot of tennis too. Being about your size I had a hard time anticipating and returning lobs. I was short but I was a fast mover. Since I was quick, I could usually run back and wait until after it bounced and then make the return." Grandma's eyes twinkled. I hoped I would be as wise as she was when I got to be her age.

As we neared her home, Grandma said, "Midori, when things seem hard, say to yourself, 'Gambatte.'"

"What does that mean?" I asked.

"Well it's a Japanese word meaning 'Don't give up' and 'hang in there'. So next week during the tennis game, remember to tell yourself 'gambatte.' It will give you a special mental boost."

That night I thought of Monday's match. I needed a win to keep my singles slot on the team. Would I be up to it?

Just as I was about to fall asleep I wondered what I'd say to Sara. Maybe I shouldn't say anything? I fell asleep still unsure about what to do.

On Monday morning I woke up feeling refreshed. Grandma's encouragement and confidence in me had raised my spirits. Maybe I could beat the other girl. I'd seen her play tennis before and she was good. Darned good. She had a strong backhand and a good lob. I knew I would be in for a stiff match.

After school on my way to the courts, I saw Sara. My heart started to beat really fast. My palms got sweaty. I still wasn't sure what to say to her. Maybe I should just let the comment slide.

As we neared the locker room, Sara said, "Ready for the big match?"

"Sure am," I said.

As I put my gear into my locker, I took a deep breath. Turning to Sara I said, "Remember last week when you called the judge a name?" I was flustered. I wasn't sure what to say next. Gambatte, I told myself.

"Yeh, no big deal," Sara said.

"Well it really hurt me," I said, trying to seem calm.

"What!? How could it hurt you? I didn't call you a 'Jap.'" Sara was getting defensive.

"You don't understand. You're white. You're cutting me down too by name-calling like that." My voice was getting louder and I could feel my face getting tighter.

"Well, that's your problem, not mine," countered Sara. "I never think of you being from some ethnic group. I just see you as my friend." Her voice started to waver. I thought she was going to cry.

"Yeh, I am your friend. But I'm also a Japanese American and I'm proud of it. I don't like hearing people make ethnic slurs." I felt scared yet strong.

I didn't want to sound pushy. "Come on. It's time to get out to the courts." I tried to smooth things over. "No hard feelings?" I offered her my hand.

Sara grabbed my hand and we shook hands. "Sorry," she mumbled. I could barely hear her.

My match was next. I could see my opponent warming up. She was tall, at least five feet eight. I was five foot one. "Well, I guess I'll just have to be quicker and tougher, I told myself."

And I was. I charged everything she threw at me, even the lobs.

It was match point. I only had one more point in order to win. My heart was in my throat, but I fought to keep my concentration. With her height, the opponent could easily fight back and quickly destroy my lead.

After returning the ball several times, I approached the net and slammed the ball cross court to my opponent's right. Barely reaching the ball, she lobbed it over my head.

Gambatte, I yelled inwardly to myself. Quickly I ran back behind the baseline. The ball bounced. Holding my racket high above my right shoulder I swung the racket down as hard as I could. The ball seemed to move in slow motion. It flew close to the net and hit right on the other side slicing to the left. My opponent raced to hit the ball, but couldn't run fast enough. I had won.

That night I called Grandma. "I won, Grandma! I won the game!"

Grandma got excited. "Congratulations! I knew you could do it," she said proudly.

"And, Grandma," I went on, "I talked to Sara about her name-calling the other day. You were so right. I feel much better now."

Grandma said gently, "I knew you had the courage to talk to Sara."

"Thanks, Grandma," I said with feeling. "I feel really great about what I can do and who I am. See you Sunday. Bye." Hanging up the phone I smiled into the large oval hall mirror, jumped up and yelled, "Gambatte!"

GLOSSARY

Japanese words are easy to say if you sound out each syllable. In most cases, each syllable gets equal emphasis.

All the consonants are pronounced as in English, and the five vowel sounds are pronounced as follows:

a—much the same as the **a** as in **father**, but a little shorter.

e—as in **yet, get, hen.**

i—as the **i** in **routine**, but somewhat shorter.

o—much the same as the **o** in **oil.**

u—most nearly like the **oo** sound in **food.**

Baachan—Endearing slang term for grandmother.
Confucius—Chinese philosopher and teacher; lived approximately 557—479 B.C.
Edo—also spelled Yedo, the old name for the city of Tokyo.
Gambatte—to persevere under adverse conditions, to try with all your strength. A rallying cry in sports or in pressure situations.
Haiku—a form of popular short Japanese poetry wih seventeen syllables, three lines in the order of 5—7—5 syllables.
Haole—Hawaiian word for white person.
Hyogo—the old name for the city of Osaka.
Issei—Japanese immigrants in the United States; first generation.
JACL—Japanese American Citizens League, the national organization for Japanese Americans.
Japantown—same as Nihonmachi, area in a city of Japanese American businesses and homes.
Jiichan—Endearing slang for grandfather.
Judo—the Japanese art of self discipline and self defense.

Kibei—A native born citizen of the United States, but educated in Japan from early childhood and returning to settle in the U.S.

Kori—a Japanese form of trunk made from woven reeds or bamboo. It was used for carrying or storing light things like clothes or flowers. In some homes with a soft lining, it was used as a bassinet for newborn infants.

Makisushi—sweet vinegared rice rolled in sea weed or egg, stuffed with colorful vegetables and sometimes sea foods or fish pro—ducts.

Maru—A traditional word at—tached to the names of Japanese commercial ships.

Nichi Bei—Japanese America; also the name of an English—Japanese newspaper, Nichi Bei Times.

Nihon machi—Literally, Japantown, area of Japanese American businesses and homes.

Nisei—A native born citizen of the United States having Issei parents; second generation.

Origami—the art and craft of forming shapes by folding square peices of colorful paper.

Osushi—same as sushi, see below.

Samurai—A Japanese warrior, or knight in ancient history.

Sansei—An American citizen born of Nisei parents; third generation.

Shinto—The ethnic religion of the Japanese consisting of reverence shown to im—perial ancestors, historical personages and to some gods of nature.

Sushi—A collection of rice dishes when the rice is flavored with sweet vinegar, cooled, and topped or rolled with vegetables and/or fresh fish and other sea foods.

Tanka—A form of short poetry simular to haiku, but longer.

Tofu—a soft white block of soy bean curd. A popular everyday protein food.

Yedo—same as Edo, the old name for Tokyo.

Yonsei—An American citizen born of Sansei parents; fourth generation.

REFERENCES

LITERATURE

Bonham, Frank. *Burma Rifles, a story of Merrill's Marauders*. New York: Thomas Y. Crowell Co., 1960

Cavanna Betty. *Jenny Kimura*. New York: William Morrow & Co., 1964

Conrat, Maisie & Richard. *Executive Order 9066, the internment of 110,000 Japanese Americans*. San Francisco: California Historical Society, 1972

Goodsell, Jane. *Daniel Inouye*. New York: Thomas Crowell, 1977

Heco, Joseph and James Murdoch, Editor. *The Narrative of a Japanese, Volume I & II*. San Francisco: American Japanese Publishing Assoc.

Houston, Jeanne W. and James. *Farewell to Manzanar*. Boston: Houghton Mifflin Company, 1973

Inouye, Daniel K. with Lawrence Elliott. *Journey to Washington*. Englewood Cliff, N.J.: Prentice-Hall, Inc., 1967.

Means, Florence Crannell. *The Moved Outers*. Boston: Houghton Mifflin Co., 1945

Okubo, Mine. *Citizen 13660*. Seattle: University of Washington Press, 1983 (reprint)

Tobias, Tobi. *Isamu Noguchi, The Life of a Sculptor*. New York: Thomas Crowell, 1974

Uchida, Yoshiko. *The Best Bad Thing*. New York: Atheneum, 1983

Uchida, Yoshiko. *The Happiest Ending*. New York: Atheneum, 1985.

Uchida, Yoshiko. *A Jar of Dreams*. New York: Atheneum, 1982

Uchida, Yoshiko. *Journey Home*. New York: Atheneum, 1978

Uchida, Yoshiko. *Journey to Topaz*. New York: Charles Scribners Sons, 1971

Uchida, Yoshiko. *Samurai of Gold Hill*. New York: Charles Scribners Sons, 1972

Uchida, Yoshiko. *Sea of Gold and Other Tales from Japan*. New York: Charles Scribners Sons, 1965

AUDIO VISUALS

JACP, INC. *Japanese Americans: An Inside Look*. Stanford: Multi Media Productions, 1974, filmstrip/cassette Multi Media Productions.

JACP, INC. *Prejudice in America: The Japanese Americans*. Stanford: Multi Media Productions, 1974, 4 filmstrips/cassettes

Okazaki, Steven. *Unfinished Business*. San Francisco: Mouchette Films, 1985

Visual Communications. *Wataridori: Birds of Passage*. Los Angeles: Visual Communications, 16mm color film

Visual Communications. *Manzanar*. Los Angeles: Visual Communications, 16mm black & white film, 20 minutes

POSTERS

1942 Japanese American Concentration Camp Photos. Documentary Photo Aids Inc.

Evacuation Notice, 1942. reproduction of originals

Issei Women. Oakland, Ca: ARC Associates

CULTURAL ACTIVITIES

Araki, Chiyo. *Origami in the Classroom, Book I: Activities for Autumn through Christmas*. Rutland, VT: Charles E. Tuttle, 1965

Araki, Chiyo. *Origami in the Classroom, Book II: Activities for Winter through Summer*. Rutland,VT: Charles E. Tuttle, 1968

Araki, Nancy K.& Jane Horii. *Matsuri! Festival!: Japanese American Celebrations and Activities*. Fremont,CA: Heian International, 1984

Honda, Isao. *World of Origami*. New York: Japan Publications, 1965

Hanafuda. *The Flower Card Game*. Tokyo: Japan Publications, 1970

Kojima, Takashi. *Japanese Abacus, Its Use and Theory*. Rutland, Vt: Charles E. Tuttle, 1954

Mikami, Takahiko. *Sumi-e Painting, Study of Japanese Brush Painting*. Tokyo:Japan Publications, 1965

Nakamura, Eiji. *Flying Origami, Origami from Pure Fun to True Science*. Tokyo:Japan Publications, 1972

Nihonmachi Little Friends. *Japanese Children's Song book & cassette*. San Francisco:Nihonmachi Little Friends, 1983

Smith, Arthur. *Game of Go, the National Game of Japan*. Rutland,Vt:Charles E. Tuttle, 1956

Streeter, Tal. *Art of Japanese Kite*. Rutland, Vt: Charles E. Tuttle, 1974

Takahama, Toshie. *Origami for Fun, 31 Basic Models*. Tokyo: Shufunotomo, 1973

Takahama, Toshie. *Joy of Origami, Ten Basic Folds Which Create Many Forms*. Tokyo: Shufunotomo, 1984

Teshigahara, Wafu. *Ikebana, A New Illustrated Guide to Mastery*. Tokyo: Japan Publications, 1981

Yamada, Sadami. *Complete Sumi-e Techniques*. Tokyo: Japan Publications, 1966

Yoneji, Noriko. *Hiragana for Fun book 1 & 2*. Tokyo: Kyobundoh Co., 1981

HISTORY

Barker, Sotera. *George Shima—"The Potato King."* Stockton, CA: Impact, 1985

Boddy, E. Manchester. *Japanese in America*. E. Manchester Boddy, Los Angeles, CA, 1921

Bosworth, Allan R. *America's Concentration Camps*. New York: W.W. Norton Co., 1967

Chuman, Frank F. *Bamboo People: The Law & Japanese Americans*. Del Mar, CA: Publishers Inc., 1979

Daniels, Roger. *Concentration Camps of North America, Japanese in the U.S. and Canada During World War II*. Malabar, Fl: Krieger Publishing, 1981

Daniels, Roger. *The Decision to Relocate the Japanese Americans*. New York: J.B. Lippincott Co., 1975

Daniels, Roger. *The Politics of Prejudice, The Anti-Japanese Movement in California and the Struggle for Japanese Exclusion*. Berkeley, Ca: University of California Press, 1977

Dillon, Richard. *Delta Country*. San Francisco: Presidio Press, 1982. Duus, Masayo. *Tokyo Rose, Orphan of the Pacific*. New York: Harper & Row, 1979

Harger, Fern. *From the Satsuma 15 to the Friends of Kagoshima*. Sonoma,Ca: Historical Museum Foundation, 1982.

Harrington, Joseph D. *Yankee Samurai, The Secret Role of Nisei in America's Pacific Victory*. Detroit: Pettigrew Enterprises, 1979

Hata, Don & Nadine. *Japanese Americans & World War II*. St. Louis,Mo: Forum Press, 1974

Herman, Masako. *Japanese in America 1843-1973*. Dobbs Ferry: Oceana Publications, 1977

Hosokawa, Bill. *JACL in Quest of Justice, The History of the Japanese American Citizens League*. New York: William Morrow & Company, Inc., 1982

Ichihashi, Yamato. *Japanese in the United States*. Arno Press, 1932

Irons, Peter. *Justice at War—The Story of the Japanese American Internment Cases*. Oxford: Oxford University Press, 1984

Japanese American Curriculum Project. *Concentration Camp USA Regulations*. San Mateo,Ca: JACP, 1943

Japanese American Curriculum Project. *Wartime Hysteria: The Role of the Press*. San Mateo,Ca: JACP, 1982

Jones, Idwal. *Vines in the Sun*. New York: Wm Morrow, 1949.

Katase, Tamon. *Rice Growing in California and How to Deal in California Rice*. Pacific Trading Co. Research Department, 1924.

Kawamura, Yusen. *Koda, Keisaburo Den*. Japan, 1965 (in Japanese).

Kitano, Harry. *Japanese Americans, the Evolution of a Subculture*. Englewood Cliff, NJ: Prentice-Hall Inc., 1976

Montero, Darrel. *Japanese Americans, Changing Patterns of Ethnic Affiliation Over Three Generations*, Boulder,Co: Westview Press, 1980

Myer, Dillon. *Uprooted Americans, the Japanese Americans and the War Relocation Authority During World War II*. Tucson, Az: University of Arizona Press, 1971

Ogawa, Dennis. *Jan Ken Po—the World of Hawaii's Japanese Americans*. Honolulu,Hi: University of Hawaii Press, 1974

Ogawa, Dennis. *Kodomo No Tame Ni, For the Sake of Our Children, the Japanese American Experience in Hawaii*. Honolulu,Hi: University of Hawaii Press, 1978

Ohashi, Kanzo. Stockton Dobashi, Tokyo, Japan. Showa 12 (in Japanese). Okazaki, Suzie Kobuchi. *Nihonmachi: A Story of San Francisco's Japantown*. San Francisco: 1985.

Saiki, Patsy. *Ganbare! An Example of Japanese Spirit*. Honolulu, Hi: Kisaku, Inc., 1982

Sarasohn, Sunada. *Issei—Portrait of a Pioneer*. Palo Alto,Ca: Pacific Books, Publishers, 1983 Sasaki, Shuichi. America Seikatsu. 1937 (in Japanese).

Tanaka, Chester. *Go For Broke, A pictorial history of the JA 100th infantry battalion & 442nd Regimental Combat Team*. Richmond,Ca: Go For Broke, Inc., 1982

Tateishi, John. *And Justice for All: An Oral History of the Japanese American Detention Camps*. New York: Random House, Inc., 1984

tenBroek, Jacobus, E. Barnhart & F. Matson. *Prejudice, War and the Constitution, Causes and Consequences of the Evacuation of the Japanese Americans in World War II*. Berkeley, Ca: University of California Press, 1954

Weglyn, Michi. *Years of Infamy, the Untold Story of America's Concentration Camps*. New York: William Morrow & Company, Inc., 1976

Wilson, Robert & Bill Hosokawa. *East to America, A History of the Japanese in the United States*. New York: Wm Morrow & Co., 1980

Yamasaki, Minoru. *A Life in Architecture*. New York: Weatherhill, 1979

Yoneda, Karl G. *Ganbatte, Sixty Year Struggle of a Kibei Worker*. Los Angeles: Asian American Studies Center,University of California, 1983

Yoshimura, Toshio. *George Shima-Potato King and Lover of Chinese Classics*. Japan, 1981.

ARTICLES AND PERIODICALS

Hawaii Herald, Japanese American monthly. Honolulu, Hi

Hokubei Mainichi, Japanese American Daily. San Francisco, Ca

Jones, Terry, *Samurai of the Wine Country: A Biography of Kanaye Nagasawa*. Pacific Citizen (Los Angeles,CA), Vol.81-No.25,December 19-26, 1975.

Nichi Bei Times, Japanese American Daily. San Francisco, Ca

Pacific Citizen, National Publication of the Japanese American Citizens League. Los Angeles, Ca

Pacific Motor Boat, *A Motor Tug Boat of the California Delta*. Dec. 1913.

Rafu Shimpo, Japanese American Daily. Los Angeles, Ca

Tozai Times, Japanese American monthly magazine. Los Angeles, Ca

*For information on available materials, send $2.00 for a current catalogue to JACP, Inc., Box 367, San Mateo, CA 94401.

ABOUT THE WRITERS

Takako Endo, BA English, poet, writer and journalist. A contributor to magazines, anthologies and other publications. Has co-authored educational books.

Florence M. Hongo, BA History, US & Asia, Secondary and Community College Credential. Post Graduate work Educational Technology. Instructor, College of San Mateo. Contributor to numerous educational publications.

Sadao Kinoshita, BA Education, MA Elementary Education, Curriculum General Elementary Credential. Teacher, Union School District, San Jose, California.

Katherine Reyes, BA Education, MA Elementary Education, General Elementary and Administrative Credentials, San Francisco Unified School District.

Donald Y. Sekimura, BS Secondary Education, BS Elementary Education. Classroom teacher, Redwood City Elementary School District, Redwood City, California.

Rosie Shimonishi, BA Education, Elementary Credential. Former Elementary teacher, Redwood City Elementary School District, Redwood City, California.

Shizue Yoshina, BA,MA, Biochemistry, General Secondary Credential. Formerly Science and Social Studies teacher, High School and Middle School in Hawaii and California.